ALSO BY MARK JONES LORENZO

Affront to Meritocracy: Stories of Overlooked Talents, Ignored Abilities, and Hidden Truths

Not Ok: A Requiem for GW-BASIC

Apophenia's Antidote: A Probability and Statistics Primer

Its Wildness Lies in Wait: Mathematical Fallacies, Cognitive Traps, and Debunking the Myths of the Lottery

The Paper Computer Unfolded: A Twenty-First Century Guide to the Bell Labs CARDIAC (CARDboard Illustrative Aid to Computation), the LMC (Little Man Computer), and the IPC (Instructo Paper Computer)

Ok: The Resurrection of GW-BASIC

ENDLESS LOOP
∞

ENDLESS LOOP

∞

The History of the BASIC Programming Language
(<u>B</u>eginner's <u>A</u>ll-purpose <u>S</u>ymbolic <u>I</u>nstruction <u>C</u>ode)

Mark Jones Lorenzo

SE BOOKS
Philadelphia | Pittsburgh

Ψ
SE BOOKS
5307 West Tyson Street
Philadelphia, Pennsylvania 19107
www.sebooks.com

Copyright © 2017 by Mark Jones Lorenzo

All rights reserved. Printed in the United States of America. No part of this book may be reproduced in any manner whatsoever without written permission except in the case of brief quotations embodied in critical articles and reviews. For information, contact SE BOOKS.

References to websites (URLs) were accurate at the time of writing. Neither the author nor SE BOOKS is responsible for URLs that may have expired or changed since the manuscript was prepared.

Published in full-throated defiance of Yog's Law.

Library cataloging information is as follows:

Lorenzo, Mark Jones
 Endless loop : the history of the BASIC programming language (Beginner's All-purpose Symbolic Instruction Code)/ Mark Jones Lorenzo.
 p. ; cm.
  Includes bibliographical references.
  I. Title
 1. Basic (computer programming language). 2. History (computers).
  QA76.19 C22 2017
  004.1396'52320—js22
  20177432194
 ISBN: 978-1-974-27707-0

10 9 8 7 6 5 4 3 2 1

Dedicated to John Kemeny and Thomas Kurtz

1964: *John Kemeny and Thomas Kurtz create BASIC, an unstructured programming language for non-computer scientists.*

1965: *Kemeny and Kurtz go to 1964.*

— James Iry, "A Brief, Incomplete, and Mostly Wrong History of Programming Languages"

CONTENTS

∞

INTRODUCTION		13
1	The Advent of Computers	19
2	Kemeny and Kurtz Arrive at Dartmouth	35
3	The Birth of Time-Sharing	43
4	The Creation of BASIC	49
5	Many Changes, Many BASICs	61
6	It's Not Small—It's Tiny BASIC	67
7	The Language of Superheroes	79
8	The Breakout Breakthrough	85
9	The Day Microsoft Almost Died	93
10	BASIC, Widely Distributed	99
11	Microsoft, IBM, and the Clones	109
12	IBM BASIC Becomes the Standard	115
13	The Twilight of Line-Numbered BASIC	121
14	BASIC Gets Structured	131
15	Kemeny and Kurtz Strike Back	149
16	The Third Generation	155
17	Thinking Small	161
END		169
RESOURCES		175
ACKNOWLEDGMENTS		187
ABOUT THE AUTHOR		189

INTRODUCTION
∞

In the early morning hours of May 1, 1964, Dartmouth College birthed fraternal twins: BASIC, the Beginner's All-purpose Symbolic Instruction Code programming language, and, simultaneously, the Dartmouth Time-Sharing System (DTSS). It hadn't been an easy birth, and the gestation period was likewise difficult. BASIC was primarily the idea of one man, mathematics professor John Kemeny, a brilliant Hungarian mathematician who had once been an assistant to Albert Einstein, while the DTSS satisfied the vision of another, mathematics and statistics professor Thomas Kurtz, who had brought a democratizing spirit to Dartmouth's campus in the form of free computing for all.

At first, Kemeny and Kurtz were worried that BASIC would be rejected. To help promote the language, BASIC was released into the public domain. BASIC and DTSS caught on at Dartmouth quickly, with a vast majority of undergraduates (and faculty) making use of the computer system via teletypewriters only several years after its inception. Other universities and even high schools connected to the DTSS; the phone company had to install new trunk lines to keep up with demand. Some institutions even copied the layout of the DTSS, making BASIC available on their own time-sharing systems. General Electric, who supplied Dartmouth with the computers to power the DTSS, monetized the setup elsewhere, becoming the largest supplier of time-sharing services within a decade.

In the early 1970s, with the personal computer revolution fast approaching, Kemeny and Kurtz began to lose control over

BASIC. The language was being adapted to run on a wide variety of computers, some much too short of memory to contain the full set of Dartmouth BASIC features. Compromises due to hardware were made early on; as hardware improved, implementations of BASIC, which were usually interpreters rather than compilers (Dartmouth BASIC was always compiled), obtained "features" that were hardware-dependent, especially in the realm of graphics. Most notably, Microsoft built its business on the back of BASIC interpreters for a variety of small computers. The microcomputers of this era usually had BASIC stored in ROM, so the machines booted up to BASIC.

By the early 1980s, personal computers—especially ones from Commodore, Tandy, and Apple as well as latecomer IBM—had replaced time-sharing, there were innumerable BASIC dialects, and standardization of the language seemed like a distant dream. Although BASIC was a popular teaching tool in schools, the language had already come under attack by such notables as computer scientist Edsger W. Dijkstra for its lack of structure. Perhaps the most cutting criticisms of BASIC, however, came from Kemeny and Kurtz, who adopted the derisive epithet "Street BASIC" to label the mass of blasphemous BASIC dialects that had proliferated. Admitting that they had underestimated the appeal of BASIC and had pushed for standardization of the language too late, Kemeny and Kurtz attempted to right the ship by releasing True BASIC, a structured BASIC (with optional vestigial line numbers) that hewed closely to the design principles of the original Dartmouth BASIC.

But by then it was too late. Although Microsoft continued to include versions of BASIC—including QBASIC, which allowed for structured programming—through later iterations of MS-DOS, BASIC practically disappeared from the computing scene overnight. Sure, Microsoft released Visual Basic and Small Basic to great acclaim, but the dominance of BASIC had long since passed.

The ascendance of BASIC paralleled the emergence of the personal computer, so the story of BASIC is first and foremost a story—actually, many interlocking stories—about computers. But it is also a tale of talented people who built a language out of a set of primal ingredients: sweat, creativity, rivalry, jealousy, cooperation, and plain hard work, and then set the language loose in a world filled with unintended consequences. How those unintended consequences played out, leading to the demise of the most popular computer language the world has ever known, is the central focus of ENDLESS LOOP.

This is not a book on how to program; rather, it is a book chronicling the history, development, and influence of a programming language. Specifically, Dartmouth BASIC, True BASIC, Tiny BASIC, Microsoft BASIC—including Altair BASIC, Applesoft BASIC, Color BASIC, Commodore BASIC, TRS-80 Level II BASIC, TI BASIC, IBM BASICA/GW-BASIC, QuickBASIC/QBASIC, Visual Basic, and Small Basic—as well as 9845 BASIC, Atari BASIC, BBC BASIC, CBASIC, Locomotive BASIC, MacBASIC, QB64, Simons' BASIC, Sinclair BASIC, SuperBASIC, and Turbo Basic/PowerBASIC, among a number of other implementations, are examined. Lines of code themselves, though sometimes necessary to flesh out the narrative or to illustrate important concepts, are used sparingly. When code does appear, it is displayed using one of two fonts: **Consolas** for first- or second-generation BASIC, or `Courier New` for third-generation BASIC. (Note that many teletypewriters printed the number "0" [zero] without a slash and the letter "O" ["oh"] with a slash, like this: Ø ; Consolas, however, does the opposite, which has become the standard since the 1980s. Slashed "oh" may have begun as part of an early mathematical convention to avoid confusing letters with digits, but it predated electronic computers by centuries. The shift from slashed "oh" to slashed zero may be due to the influence of IBM's SHARE organization of the 1950s, which was an IBM 704 mainframe users' association that adopted the practice.) Technical terms and abbreviations are explained when they are first used in the text. While a familiarity with some form of BASIC is advantageous, not being fluent in the programming language—or in any programming language, for that matter—is not an impediment to understanding.

Before telling the story of BASIC, however, we need to take a step back to tell an even bigger one: the advent of computers.

ENDLESS LOOP
∞

CHAPTER 1

∞

The Advent of Computers

Computers, in one form or another, have been around since the dawn of humankind. There is no requirement that computers be digital—or even electronic. Here is the difference: a digital device converts an input into, usually, binary information, whereas an analog device can handle a range of inputs (for example, think of a record player or even a non-electronic thermostat).

Stonehenge, the monument in Wiltshire, England, was perhaps the world's first computer. More than just a haphazard arrangement of large stones, Stonehenge allowed ancient humans to make astronomical predictions, with a little help from the sun and the stars.

The digits on our hands help us count and perform the simplest of calculations—likely spurring the development of the base 10 numbering system (although in ancient times there were other bases in circulation, such as the Babylonian's base 60, or sexagesimal). Eventually, having run out of fingers, human beings substituted rocks and sticks to stand in for quantities until even those physical stand-ins were abstracted away in favor of symbols. Calculations with these symbols soon followed.

The use of mechanical aids for calculation goes back thousands of years. Consider the abacus, likely developed by the Chinese (although the abacus might originally have come from the Middle East). Also consider the Antikythera mechanism, an analog device, which was built for astronomical predictions. Mathematician John

Napier, who invented logarithms—in effect turning multiplication into addition—also invented a set of analog numbering rods that came to be known as Napier's Bones; if not for logarithms, the slide rule, also an analog device, would never have been developed.

During the Renaissance, a young Blaise Pascal invented an adding machine to help his father who worked as a tax farmer (what we would call a tax collector today). By the time he was a teenager, Pascal had improved the adding machine, which he had patented, enabling it to perform multiplication and division as well. Another mathematician from the Renaissance, Gottfried Wilhelm Leibniz, who co-invented calculus along with Isaac Newton, improved on Pascal's design, calling his updated machine a "step reckoner." Leibniz's step reckoner died a quick death, though, because of its high production costs.

Look up the word "computer" in dictionaries from as late as the first half of the twentieth century, and definitions will invariably refer to *people* who compute, not machines. Despite the calculating machines of Pascal and Leibniz, "computers"—i.e., "human calculators"—performed most of the calculations for the logarithmic and trigonometric tables that were important for engineering, astronomical, and mathematical calculations during the Renaissance. Even in World War II centuries later, there were still a large share of (human) computers, mainly women, busily calculating numbers for ballistics' firing tables and helping to piece together an atomic bomb.

The first person to design a functional, though only posthumously built, computer was Charles P. Babbage. Babbage, born the son of a London banker, was a professor of mathematics at Cambridge University in the nineteenth century. Frustrated with the errors that he kept encountering with hand-calculated mathematical tables, he sketched out the Difference Engine (to solve polynomial equations) and the Analytical Engine (an advanced tabulator and computer). The Analytical Engine was programmable: Babbage used a sophisticated punched card system, repurposed from the Jacquard loom sewing machine developed by Joseph Marie Jacquard.

Ada Lovelace, the daughter of poet Lord Byron, was Babbage's epistolary collaborator for a number of years before her death; she began corresponding with the professor when she was only seventeen. Her mother, Lady Anne Isabella Milbanke Byron—who left her husband Lord Byron soon after Ada was born—had Ada tutored in logic and mathematics, not because she believed in her daughter's abilities in the subjects per se, but because she wanted to ensure that her daughter wouldn't take after her father in any way. Many people consider Lovelace the world's first computer programmer because she contributed a lengthy *Notes* addendum to a published article by Louis Menabrea on the Analytical Engine (she had translated the piece from Italian to English), specifically describing methods of programming the device. In her *Notes*, the first programming loop is proffered as well as a program for calculating Bernoulli numbers. Lovelace also foresaw a variety of interesting applications for the computer, such as with music: "[s]upposing, for instance, that the fundamental relations of pitched sounds in the science of harmony and of musical composition were susceptible of such expression and adaptations, the [Analytical] Engine might compose elaborate and scientific pieces of music of any degree of complexity or extent," she wrote.

Babbage received sufficient funding from the British government to construct his machines, which required the fashioning of thousands of gears and other moving parts, but insufficient tooling technology made them physically impossible to build at the time. Nonetheless, the idea of programming and storing information via punched cards was a good one, ultimately becoming the standard for electronic computers over a century later.

The American inventor Herman Hollerith put the punched-card concept into practice in the late nineteenth century. Hollerith worked at the U.S. Census Bureau; by the 1890 census, millions of punched cards had been utilized to compile demographic statistics, completing the census in record time thanks to his innovations. Later, Hollerith founded the Tabulating Machine Company, specializing in tabulating equipment, which was consolidated in the 1920s to form International Business Machines (IBM). The standardized 80-column punched cards that IBM introduced in 1928, sometimes referred to as Hollerith cards or simply IBM cards, were the antecedent to the 80-column displays—with 80 characters per row—of time-sharing terminals and monitors as well as later personal computers such as the Commodore PET 8000 series.

Those early-model automated calculating machines used by U.S. census takers were neither digital nor programmable. The 1920s brought Lehmer sieves, large machines that could factor mathematical expressions. Lehmer sieves were electronic, but relied on a mass of chains, switches, and gears. Shortly before World War II, the lauded American engineer and inventor Vannevar Bush constructed a "differential analyzer," which was a differential equation-solving mechanical analog computer, while the German engineer Konrad Zuse built the Z1, a simple programmable computer, in his parents' apartment.

During World War II, though, computers began to come into their own, laying the groundwork for what Alvin Toffler later called "future shock": an incredible amount of change in a terribly short period of time. There was the electromechanical Harvard Mark I Computer, also called the Automatic Sequence Controlled Calculator, built by Howard Aiken at Harvard University. Aiken's impetus for constructing the computer was one of necessity: he had to complete extensive calculations for his doctoral thesis. But Aiken realized that such a machine could be more than a one-trick pony, so he wrote a proposal to IBM for help with its construction. In the proposal, Aiken noted that increased computational power drove scientific progress; he explained how the Mark I, which used cards and paper tape for input, would be able to handle an array of mathematical operations, such as powers, logarithms, grouping symbols, trigonometric functions, hyperbolic functions, real roots (i.e., numerical solutions) to equations, and even numerical integration and differentiation.

The outbreak of the Second World War initially interfered with plans to build the machine. But by 1944 the Mark I was finally completed and turned over to Aiken, who continued to serve in the Navy for the remainder of the war. Grace Hopper, who had a doctorate in mathematics from Yale and would eventually rise to the rank of admiral before she left the military, was assigned to assist Aiken with the computer's operation. Hopper helped to popularize the term "bug" in computing: after she excised a dead moth that was blocking a relay and paper tape, Hopper said she had "debugged" the program.

The Mark I was adapted to solve war-related mathematical problems, including those related to radar design and the atomic bomb. The Navy, not completely satisfied with the Mark I, commissioned a second computer, the Mark II, which Aiken also designed. After the war, two more models were built—the Mark III and the Mark IV—but they operated slowly.

The Mark I had been designed to use vacuum tubes, the precursor to transistors and the microchips of today. But costs and time constraints instead resulted in a machine with many moving parts: punched tape (for program storage, fed into the machine), mechanical relays (on-off switches controlled by electric currents), adding accumulators, and switches. The more moving parts in a machine, the higher the probability of a breakdown, thus making such electromechanical computers far from ideal. Things had to change.

Setting the stage for that change, albeit indirectly, was George Boole. He was born in England in 1815, the same year as Ada Lovelace. Boole, with a bit of help from his father, taught himself mathematics and classical languages; he was appointed a professor of mathematics in Ireland. His subspecialty of interest, though, was mathematical logic. In *Laws of Thought*, Boole described his Boolean algebra, in which he said that mathematics, not language, was the key to systemizing logic; Boole even believed that this systemization could shed light on the inner workings of the human brain. Ultimately, we can pare down Boolean algebra, and the operations performed with it, to just two operands: 0 (off/false) and 1 (on/true). Since within their circuits digital computers operate using Boolean algebra and thus binary logic, George Boole was critical to the development of the computer. Boole didn't realize the import of his ideas but neither did Babbage, despite corresponding with him.

There are two people most responsible for the shift from electromechanical computers to digital, electronic, programmable computers. The first is Alan Turning, a British mathematician. He was born in 1912 in London and showed an early aptitude in mathematics, enrolling at the University of Cambridge and later earning his doctorate at Princeton University under the direction of renowned mathematician Alonzo Church. At Princeton, Turing studied cryptology, which came in handy during the Second World War when, after returning to Cambridge, he was recruited to work at Bletchley Park to help decode the German Enigma machine. Turing's team utilized the Colossus series of computers, created by British engineer Tommy Flowers, to successfully crack the Enigma.

Besides the famous Turing test, which helps ascertain if a machine exhibits sufficiently human-like behaviors, Alan Turing's most lasting contribution to the field of computing is his concept of the Universal Turing machine (UTM), first presented in the 1936 paper entitled "On Computable Numbers, with an Application to the *Entscheidungsproblem*." In the piece, Turing discusses computable and non-computable numbers, an open problem by the mathematician David Hilbert, the halting problem, and the aforementioned Turing machines.

David Hilbert believed that all formal mathematical systems could be made both consistent and complete—that is, have an exhaustive set of axioms. This formalization program became his life's work. Mathematicians Alfred North Whitehead and Bertrand Russell were in support of Hilbert's Program, publishing a multi-volume work called *Principia Mathematica* (1910-1913) that sought to place mathematics on a firm, unshakable foundation. But Hilbert's Program nearly collapsed in 1931 thanks to Kurt Gödel and his incompleteness theorems. Gödel managed to prove that any mathematical system cannot be both consistent and complete; there will always be statements unprovable within the system.

In the 1979 masterwork *Gödel, Escher, Bach*, author Douglas Hofstadter presents the analogy of a heavy rope being used to connect two seafaring ships: "first a light arrow is fired across the gap, pulling behind it a thin rope. Once a connection has been established between the two ships this way, then the heavy rope can be pulled across the gap." The thin rope represents mathematical proofs "employing a very restricted set of principles of reasoning...." Hofstadter explains that "Gödel showed that in order to pull the heavy rope across the gap, you can't use a lighter rope; there just isn't a strong enough one." Restated, Gödel demonstrated that any consistent axiomatic mathematical system must include undecidable propositions—propositions that can neither be proven true nor false. *Principia Mathematica* was dead in the water.

Alonzo Church and Alan Turing put the final nails in the coffin of Hilbert's Program, courtesy of providing an answer to the *Entscheidungsproblem*, or decision problem, which is as follows: Does there exist an algorithm that can *always* determine if a mathematical statement is true? (Hilbert phrased the decision problem this way: "The *Entscheidungsproblem* is solved when one knows a procedure by which one can decide in a finite number of operations whether a given logical expression is generally valid or is satisfiable.") Using different approaches, both Church and Turing answered the *Entscheidungsproblem* in the negative: i.e., there is no such algorithm.

Turing sketched out a theoretical construct called a Turing machine to prove it.

A Turing machine is a finite-state machine (there are a countable number of states) that is fed a long paper tape beneath a read-write head. The paper tape has squares containing symbols, such as 0 or 1, which store the inputs or outputs of calculations, but the squares on the tape can be blank, too. A Turing machine can erase or overwrite a symbol, change its state, halt, or perform a combination of these actions, all depending on the paper tape—which, of course, contains the program, which Turing called the "instruction set."

Turing realized that these finite-state Turing machines are able to completely model the *entire* universe of computing possibilities; essentially, the operations of every computer conceived can be reduced to at least one Turing machine. A computer, even a programming language, is deemed "Turing Complete" if it can do everything that a Turing machine can do. And any instruction set that can be run by a Turing machine can also be run by a Universal Turing machine, meaning that a UTM can be programmed to act as if it is a series of Turing machines simultaneously.

But Turing wasn't done yet. Consider the set of all irrational numbers, or numbers that cannot be written as either fractions or decimals which have predictable patterns. Some irrational numbers, such as π (the ratio of a circle's circumference to its diameter, with the decimal expansion of 3.14159…), have finite instruction sets that can run on the UTM to produce as many digits of the number as desired. These are the computable numbers mentioned in the title of Turing's paper. But Turing also proved that there are infinitely many other irrational numbers that, no matter the instruction set fed into the UTM, are not computable to any nth decimal place; these are the non-computable numbers.

Now consider the "halting problem," which asks, Will a program stop on its own, or slip into an endless loop? Turing classified the halting problem as "undecidable," taking a page from Gödel's work, meaning that it cannot be proven true or false: there is no finite algorithm that can *always* determine if a program halts (terminates) or slips into an endless loop. Since the halting problem *itself* is a member of the non-computable set of functions, and thus undecidable, Turing (and Alonzo Church by a different method called the lambda calculus) was able answer Hilbert's *Entscheidungsproblem*, his decision problem—thus forever halting Hilbert's Program. (To summarize the result, we use the catchall term "Church-Turing thesis": any calculable function is computable by using a Turing machine. Instead of using a UTM, Hofstadter describes a computer language called "GlooP" that *can* in fact be programmed to compute the non-computable, but then he proceeds to rigorously demonstrate that "GlooP" cannot exist after all, confirming the Church-Turing thesis.)

Besides Alan Turing, the other person most responsible for the shift from electromechanical computers to digital, electronic, programmable computers is the Hungarian mathematician John von Neumann. Von Neumann acquired the "von" when his banker father was gifted a heredity title; despite young John showing a strong aptitude in mathematics and languages, his father attempted to steer his son away from studying math. But John von Neumann persisted, eventually earning a doctorate in mathematics from the University of Budapest.

At first, von Neumann had little interest in computers. He took university lecturer posts, wrote papers with David Hilbert, and published copious numbers of works on set theory, game theory, and logic. He landed at the Institute for Advanced Study in Princeton, where Albert Einstein was in residence. Von Neumann was then recruited to join the Manhattan Project, which was tasked with secretly building the atomic bomb during World War II.

After the war ended, von Neumann's interest in computers was piqued by the ENIAC (Electronic Numerical Integrator and Computer), built in the late 1940s by John Mauchly and John Eckert at the University of Pennsylvania. The ENIAC operated in decimal, not binary, its physical components barely squeezing into several large rooms; the vacuum tubes, used in place of electromechanical relays, quickly burned out, leading to frequent interruptions in calculations. But the computer had no moving parts that could wear down or break. There were ENIAC variants such as the binary EDVAC and the UNIVAC, the first electronic computer used for the census. (The EDVAC later became famous when CBS featured the machine on a television show projecting the presidential election results of 1952.) Von Neumann modified the ENIAC and also designed a computer of his own at the Institute for Advanced Study. His computer was a binary machine that stored program instructions and data in the same unit—a design that later came to be called a von Neumann architecture, which most computers have today (the Mark I did not have a von Neumann architecture, since program instructions and data were stored in different places). Von Neumann formalized his hardware design in the published *First Draft of a Report on the EDVAC* (1945).

The next computing breakthrough came at Bell Labs. Bell Telephone Laboratories was formed in the 1920s, the result of a decades-prior merger between Alexander Graham Bell's American Telephone and Telegraph Company (AT&T) and the Western Electric Company. Western established a research lab that was spun off and renamed Bell Labs; at first only stationed in New York City, Bell Labs expanded to facilities in Murray Hill, New Jersey, as well.

Bell Labs was the birthplace of the future. The laser, the solar battery, radio astronomy, the C programming language, fiber-optic transatlantic cable—all were invented there. But perhaps the most important invention to emerge from Bell Labs was the transistor.

Following World War II, Bell Labs engineer William Shockley hired Walter Brattain and John Bardeen to investigate the properties of semiconductors. Shockley initially believed that he alone had successfully designed a silicon semiconductor amplifier, but to no avail: his "field effect" theory didn't pass muster. So, Shockley assigned Brattain and Bardeen to work on the theory. Several years later, Brattain and Bardeen arrived at a solution: the point-contact transistor, completely unlike Shockley's earlier approach. Angry that they had solved the problem without needing his assistance, Shockley secretly got to work improving Brattain and Bardeen's design; a short time later, Shockley unveiled the junction (or sandwich) transistor.

Although all three men were awarded Nobel Prizes for their efforts, Shockley was ostracized at Bell Labs and had to leave. He founded a company, Shockley Semiconductor, the first of the major high-tech firms to populate Silicon Valley. But his ineffectual and abrasive management style alienated his employees, and eight of them—known as the "traitorous eight"—left to form their own company: Fairchild Semiconductor. Eventually, Bob Noyce and Gordon Moore, two of the original traitorous eight, left Fairchild to form yet another company, Intel Corporation. Of course, Moore is best known for Moore's Law, his prediction of the exponential increase in computing power coupled to ever-decreasing cost. Noyce, along with Jack Kilby of Texas Instruments, built the first integrated circuits, or microchips, which miniaturized a computer's central processing unit (CPU) onto a single chip: a wafer of silicon etched with thousands upon thousands of transistors.

Besides a CPU, no computer can do very much without memory. There is a complex hierarchy of memory storage in modern computers, but for simplicity's sake memory can be split into two basic categories: read-only memory (ROM), which is permanent, persistent, and nonvolatile, and random access memory (RAM), which is temporary, non-persistent, and volatile. Even if power is lost, data needs to remain intact; this is the purpose of ROM, of which there are several varieties—from less to more immutable: PROM to EPROM to EEPROM. Paper tape and punched cards are examples of persistent memory, as are magnetic storage devices like floppy disks and cassette tapes; magnetic cores (made of ferromagnetic and ceramic material) and tubes of mercury are also classified as persistent. By contrast, RAM is considered volatile memory since continuous power is required to keep the contents of the data intact. For instance, dynamic random access memory (DRAM) contains many memory cells; each of these memory cells has an address located at the intersection of a bitline (column) and a wordline (row). In addition, each memory cell has a transistor and a capacitor that can be set to zero by emptying a "bucket" of electrons or set to one by filling a "bucket" of electrons. Memory leaks may occur if DRAM isn't continually refreshed by a memory controller while the computer is operational. (When a computer is switched on, RAM memory cells are assigned arbitrary zeros or ones by mere chance alone.)

Poet T. S. Eliot wrote, "What we call the beginning is often the end." Software needs to be loaded by other software, but where does it begin? How is there not infinite regress? In other words, what loads that *initial* piece of software into a computer when the machine is turned on? That task is assigned to a bootloader program; the bootloader lifts the computer up by its own bootstraps, so to speak. Modern bootloaders—which load the operating system and other system software into memory—are usually stored into nonvolatile ROM and permit the computer to boot, or self-start. Early computers loaded bootloaders via punched cards or magnetic tape; many decades ago, booting on an IBM computer was referred to as an Initial Program Load (IPL), the machine starting up by loading the contents of punched cards via input.

There has to be some way for the user to communicate with a computer. High-level computer languages such as COBOL (COmmon Business-Oriented Language, developed in part by Grace Hopper, is an especially English-like language primarily used for data processing), FORTRAN (FORmula TRANslation, commonly used for scientific and mathematical purposes), ALGOL (ALGOrithmic Language, an early influential language), and Ada (named after Ada Lovelace and originally developed for the United States Department of Defense) permit the user to communicate via English-style words and phrases as well as with mathematical functions. The keywords and syntax of high-level computer languages must be unambiguous and consistent and concrete, devoid of the multiple meanings and idiomatic expressions frequently encountered in spoken languages. Regardless, a computer cannot understand the statements expressed in a high-level language without a special translator, called a compiler. A compiler converts high-level programs into a machine language that can be directly "understood" by the computer's processor. An interpreter also translates high-level code into machine code but unlike a compiler—which produces standalone executable files from high-level code—a program written with an interpreter always requires the interpreter in order to run.

At a minimum, though, what do we need in order to communicate with a computer? Recall that a Turing machine has only a few possible instructions: read or write a single symbol, halt the machine, move the paper tape left or right. Yet a Turing machine is sufficient to work through any mathematically computable problem. If we built a small computer containing only a handful of memory cells—each memory cell with its data, packaged together as a "word," would contain an address as well as a "pointer" to another address in memory—what instructions would we need? A halt instruction, to stop the machine; a load instruction, to read values stored in memory cells or input; and a store instruction, to store data into memory cells, are all required. These three instruction codes, also called operation codes (opcodes), form a simplistic instruction set that our small computer's central processing unit (CPU) can carry out—one "word" at a time. By also attaching an accumulator, which is a register that stores arithmetic operations, to our computer, we can include two more instructions, add and subtract—which will add or subtract, respectively, a value stored in a memory cell with the contents of the accumulator.

But we're not done yet. Right now, there's no flexibility; we can only run a program through our small computer address by address in a strictly sequential manner. Therefore, we need to include a jump instruction; jump will allow us to unconditionally jump to any address we wish. To add even more flexibility, let's also include a call instruction, which unconditionally jumps to a specified address but stores the address before the jump for future use, and a return instruction that returns control of the program at that stored address. Additionally, we'll add to our instruction set a conditional jump—a jump that only occurs if a specified condition is met.

Instead of using numbers to represent opcodes we can use mnemonics, such as STO for store or ADD for add or JMP for an unconditional jump. In general, we adhere to this format:

Mnemonic [destination],[source]

where both [destination] and [source] refer to memory addresses.

There are several other commonly used mnemonics worth mentioning here: PUSH and POP. These instructions are used with "stacks," a way of allocating memory. Think of a single stack of cafeteria trays, where we are only permitted to add a tray to the top of the stack or take off the tray last put on top. This idea is neatly summarized with the acronym LIFO: last in, first out. To put an element on the top of the stack, we push it on; to take off the topmost element, we pop it off the stack. A "stack overflow" error means that the stack has grown too large for memory to support. (In *Gödel, Escher, Bach*, Hofstadter illustrates the recursive nature of stacks by having the reader imagine a busy executive who keeps having to put caller after caller on hold, leading to a nested set of conversations that are "popped" off the stack by the executive, one by one.)

With the aforementioned set of mnemonics, we've built a machine language for the computer (albeit using abbreviations human beings can easily understand, rather than strings of numbers). Each microprocessor has a unique machine language, but most microprocessors have at least the same basic instruction set described above. Machine language programming on computers such as the

ENIAC was a laborious, physically demanding process that required a strong attention to detail; plug board wiring and function tables were necessary, with many wires inserted and dials turned to program only a single instruction. As the stored-program computer evolved, programming in machine code—at the level of the processor—got easier but never became easy. In his book *Code* (2001), Charles Petzold observes that writing in machine language is "like eating with a toothpick. The bites are so small and the process so laborious that dinner takes forever."

Rather than coding at the level of zeros and ones or data words, where the user is explicitly required to set memory locations for data via addresses, assembly language—where such memory management can be performed behind the scenes—emerged as an alternative means of programming a computer. Now, instead of

Mnemonic [destination],[source]

the command for our simple computer can be shortened to

Mnemonic [operand]

where [operand] is a label or reference to another command, rather than a specific memory address. Better yet, assembly language, unlike machine language, permits variables. A variable is no more than a convenient shorthand for storing data: declare a variable by name and assign it a value, which can be retrieved later on by calling the variable's name. The assembler automatically stores the variable's contents into an available address. But unlike machine code, which can be "understood" by the computer directly, assembly code requires an assembler to translate the source-code file into an executable file, readable by the machine. (Note that the aforementioned machine and assembly language discussion applies only to a small single-accumulator computer, not to more complex varieties of computers.)

Eventually, as transistors replaced vacuum tubes, high-level languages were built on the shoulders of assembly languages. High-level languages abstracted away even more from the user, allowing readable English-like commands and functions. John W. Backus, who in the 1950s led the IBM group that developed FORTRAN (originally called the IBM Mathematical FORmula TRANslating

System), the first high-level language, recalled the difficulties of programming prior to the advent of high-level languages:

> Before 1954 almost all programming was done in machine language or assembly language. Programmers rightly regarded their work as a complex, creative art that required human inventiveness to produce an efficient program. Much of their effort was devoted to overcoming the difficulties created by the computers of the era: the lack of index registers, the lack of built-in floating point [decimal] operations, restricted instruction sets..., and primitive input-output arrangements.

Backus enumerated a number of reasons why FORTRAN was developed: the inefficiency of so-called automatic programming, a way of sidestepping programming on an actual machine in favor of coding on a "synthetic," or virtual, computer using pseudocode; the high costs associated with employing many programmers; the time spent debugging programs; the development of the IBM 704, which had built-in floating-point operations; and even laziness. "Much of my work has come from being lazy," he admitted. "I don't like writing programs, and so, when I was working on the IBM 701 (an early computer), writing programs for computing missile trajectories, I started work on a programming system to make it easier to write programs."

Though influenced by the automatic programming systems of the time, especially by Laning and Zierler's algebraic system, FORTRAN was developed independently by IBM. "As far as we were aware, we simply made up the language as we went along," Backus said. He and his officially designated "Programming Research Group" believed the design of the language was secondary to a larger concern: the coding of an efficient compiler (or, as it was called then, a "translator"), which could take high-level language statements and convert them into optimized IBM 704 machine language. After a frustrating and intense couple of years, Backus and his group succeeded in their key goal: writing a language that "would make it possible for engineers and scientists to write programs for themselves on the 704." Whereas machine and assembly language were indecipherable without knowledge of computer hardware, FORTRAN was the first programming language that resembled algebra more than computerized hieroglyphics.

A single statement in any high-level language may represent dozens or even hundreds of commensurate assembly commands (e.g., FORTRAN reduced the number of coding statements necessary by at least a factor of twenty); after all, this was high-level languages' *raison d'être*: a means of shortcutting recurring groups of assembly code. And unlike assembly or machine code, high-level languages are relatively consistent from computer to computer and thus not hardware dependent, assuming functional compilers (or interpreters) were written for the languages. High-level languages permit complex programming constructions such as user-created variable types, arrays (i.e., variables treated as homogenous groups, systematically indexed), subroutines (routines grouped in blocks of code that can be called from the main program), and recursion (code that calls itself). In addition, control statements—such as conditionals and loops—are allowed. (Interestingly, Backus has said that "[w]hat FORTRAN did primarily was to mechanize the organization of loops.")

Of course, contemporary computers have user-friendly means of input: keyboard, mouse, voice. Keyboards weren't always hooked up to display monitors, however; in the 1960s and early 1970s, "keyboards" were hybrid typewriter-printers called Teletypes (technically teletypewriters, since "Teletype" also refers to the Teletype Corporation's set of teleprinters; but Teletype became a proprietary eponym akin to Kleenex and Xerox, and will be used that way throughout this book; eventually IBM, not just Teletype, produced terminals, such as the 1050 and the 2741) that printed out user-typed text and computer prompts on paper rolls and even had optional paper tape readers—to read programs stored as punched holes on paper tape—and writers—so paper tape copies of programs could be generated for later use—built-in. (Note that by the 1970s terminals could also be hooked up to display monitors, like the IBM 3270 Information Display or the Teletype Model 40 KDP—Keyboard Display Printer—Terminal.)

These Teletypes had glyphs on keys that typewriters didn't have, such as BREAK (interrupts the current operation), REPT (repetition of a character), and RUBOUT (a non-printing character, which usually deleted the last character that was typed) as well as glyphs in common with typewriters, such as SHIFT (although not for lower-case letters, of which there were none; the shift key was utilized to access additional characters and commands). In addition, many

Teletypes had rotary telephone dials and other special user controls. Most of the time, the computers these Teletypes connected to weren't even in the same room—or building. As batch processing (one program run at a time, sequentially; a program consisted of a stack of punch cards that had to be encoded offline using a key punch machine; these stacks of cards were then "fed" into a computer's input hopper in batches) gave way to time-sharing systems (optimized use of a central computer by multiple users running programs nearly simultaneously), Teletype terminals were connected to time-sharing systems via direct line or telephone (courtesy of a data set or an acoustic coupler). For instance, in *BASIC Programming and Applications* (1976), author C. Joseph Sass describes the process of connecting to a time-sharing system with the popular Teletype Model ASR33:

> In the case of [a direct line connection], to connect the terminal to the computer the user simply depresses the ORIG [standing for "originate"] key and proceeds to sign-on.... For [the data set connection], it is necessary to press the ORIG key and dial the telephone number of the computer system. The system normally answers with a high-pitched sound, and the sign-on procedure continues. (However, a telephone busy signal may be encountered. In this case, depress the CLR key, wait a few minutes, and try dialing again.)....
>
> With an acoustic coupler, the terminal must be activated and the telephone number dialed. When the computer responds with the high-pitched sound, the receiver must be placed in the acoustic coupler and the sign-on procedure completed.

Depending on the time-sharing system, you might have to type **GO** and press RETURN (which produces a carriage return/line feed on the terminal), or you may have to press CTRL and C and then the RETURN key. The system will type out an acknowledgement character: perhaps a pound sign (#), as was standard on the Michigan Terminal System (MTS), or a period (.). Next, a sign on is required: perhaps by typing **SIGNON** (MTS) and a user number, or **LOGIN** and a user number; in addition, entry of a password may be necessary.

Once signed on, you are all set to program—in BASIC.

CHAPTER 2

∞

Kemeny and Kurtz Arrive at Dartmouth

If not for director Steven Spielberg's father, BASIC might never have been developed.

From as far back as he could remember, Arnold Spielberg was interesting in tinkering with electronics. Before he was ten years of age, Spielberg was taking apart radio equipment. After the Second World War, he began building vacuum tube computers for the Radio Corporation of America (RCA). In 1957, Spielberg was hired at General Electric (GE) by engineer Homer R. "Barney" Oldfield; Spielberg was tasked with establishing GE's Industrial Computer Department in Phoenix, Arizona.

Unlike Oldfield, though, the CEO of GE, Ralph Cordiner, was completely opposed to building computers for businesses. Cordiner had a decidedly old-school mindset; he believed that GE should stick to its roots: making industrial products. Despite not having the CEO's approval, Oldfield assigned Spielberg a project: build a commercial computer. In 1959, the GE-225 was ready; it was a massive machine, with thousands of transistors and circuit boards, storing data both on paper and magnetic tape. The computer also permitted access to nearly a dozen terminals.

Bank of America was impressed, so they purchased the computer at a cost of $250,000. Cordiner attended the computer's dedication ceremony and then turned around and fired Oldfield. Although Cordiner wanted to backtrack and extricate GE from this new business, the market had other plans: GE couldn't build their computers fast enough to satisfy the demand. One GE computer ended up being used to predict the results of the 1964 U.S. presidential election; another was purchased by the Cleveland Browns football team to coordinate ticket sales. Spielberg left GE in 1963, just missing the group from Dartmouth that had arrived to learn all about the machine. How individuals from Dartmouth College, a small Ivy League liberal arts institution in Hanover, New Hampshire, came to be interested in the GE-225 is a long and circuitous story. But it all begins with two men: John George Kemeny and Thomas Eugene Kurtz.

John Kemeny possessed one of the finest mathematical minds in an age that brought us some of the best in history, such as Turing and von Neumann. Born in Budapest, Hungary, on May 31, 1926, his talents were apparent immediately, but, he and his family being Jewish, Kemeny's father, Tibor, realized early on the existential dangers ahead. Tibor tried to convince everyone in the family to immigrate to America, which he had connections to courtesy of his job as an import-export wholesaler. Most of the family left Hungary, but nearly too late: their possessions didn't make it in time. And several family members, including Kemeny's grandfather, an aunt, and an uncle, refused to leave Hungary, and died in the Holocaust.

Kemeny's ear for mathematics and language helped him to quickly acclimate to his new environment. Arriving in New York City at 13 years old without knowing a word of English, he quickly picked it up and managed to graduate from George Washington High School in three years flat—first in his class, no less. Princeton University came calling; Kemeny enrolled, majoring in mathematics. But then World War II intervened. At 18 years old Kemeny had to take off about a year from college, but he received a plum war assignment in line with his prodigious talents: working for Nobel-winning physicist and polymath Richard Feynman at Los Alamos in the theoretical division of the Manhattan Project. Kemeny would be one of the two-dozen human "computers," working through solutions to atomic bomb-related differential equations. Punch cards with IBM calculators were employed; the sheer physicality of the process, which involved repeated plug board rewiring and cycling punch cards between machines, was time-consuming and intense and had to be checked and rechecked for errors. Decades later, when punch cards were finally put to pasture, Kemeny was overjoyed, saying it was one of the happiest days of his life.

Security was understandably tight at Los Alamos. In his memoir *"Surely You're Joking, Mr. Feynman!"* (1985), Feynman—who was fascinated with testing security measures at the site, going as far as to pick locks containing bomb secrets—relays an anecdote involving his young charge:

> I also got through a letter that told about how one of the boys who worked in one of my groups, John Kemeny, had been wakened up in the middle of the night and grilled with lights in front of him by some idiots in the army there because they found out something about his father, who was supposed to be a communist or something. Kemeny is a famous man now.

Before he left Los Alamos after the war, Kemeny attended a lecture von Neumann delivered at the facility. Kemeny and von Neumann had a lot in common: both Jewish, both Hungarian, both gifted in mathematics. Von Neumann, who was contracted by the U.S. government as a consultant to the atomic bomb project, gave a memorable lecture to the Los Alamos staff about his far-flung ideas of the von Neumann architecture, describing a future populated with electronic, binary computers. (Kemeny transcribed von Neumann's lecture for his book *Man and the Computer* many years later, relaying his incredulousness upon hearing von Neumann's talk while hoping that he would live long enough to see von Neumann's ideas come to fruition. In *Man and the Computer*, Kemeny also extolled the virtues of using computers for purely recreational purposes.)

Kemeny returned to Princeton to complete his undergraduate work. And, as he had done in high school, Kemeny finished his studies in a scant three years, receiving undergraduate degrees in philosophy and mathematics. He immediately began his doctorate at Princeton under thesis advisor Alonzo Church. In the late 1940s, as he was completing his dissertation in mathematics, Kemeny worked as Albert Einstein's research assistant at the Institute for Advanced Study. Kemeny said he was invaluable to the most famous scientist of the twentieth century because "Einstein wasn't very good at math." (Einstein was deeply engrossed in unified field theory when Kemeny assisted him.) Kemeny also ran into von

Neumann at the Institute occasionally; von Neumann was busy building a computer but still found the time to have lengthy talks with Kemeny. A *Scientific American* article Kemeny published in 1955 combined the computing ideas of von Neumann, especially from the elder Hungarian's lectures at Princeton, with Turing's UTM concept.

Kemeny's contact with von Neumann continued until Kemeny, who had been teaching mathematics and philosophy, left Princeton in 1953. As a consultant for the RAND Corporation in Santa Monica, California, in 1953, Kemeny was able to—at least slightly—put into practice the advanced computing ideas he had written about in *Scientific American* by programming a clone of the computer von Neumann designed at Princeton. However, after only several months at RAND, Kemeny decided to leave for a teaching opportunity at Dartmouth College. But there was no computer on campus at Dartmouth when Kemeny arrived. That would have to wait.

Kemeny would go on to chair the Dartmouth mathematics department before turning 30 years old, developing new curricula and classes such as the freshman-only Finite Mathematics course, designed to include modern mathematical topics like matrix algebra and logic. (Why should math be "the only subject you can study for 14 years and not learn a single thing that has been done since 1800?" he asked.)

Don Morrison, dean of the faculty at Dartmouth, thought the world of John Kemeny even before he met him: Albert W. Tucker, chair of the math department at Princeton, had recommended to Morrison that he hire Kemeny—who had in turn been recommended as a top-flight talent to Tucker by Einstein, von Neumann, and Princeton undergrads whom Kemeny had taught; von Neumann said that Dartmouth "would not be making a mistake in taking Kemeny." Kemeny's bona fides beyond reproach, Morrison gave his new department chair a mission: revamp and rebuild the entire mathematics department, which at the time had an inordinately large number of faculty near-retirement, garnering it a world-class reputation in the process.

When Kemeny arrived at Dartmouth, the mathematics department wasn't particularly research-oriented. But the mathematics department faculty quickly realized that Kemeny brought the winds of change. Right before he became department chairman, Kemeny attended his first math department faculty meeting, interjecting that a secretary needed to be hired to work exclusively with the department. "Well, I don't think we need a secretary," a fellow faculty member piped up. "When we have a paper to type, we take it down to Mrs. So and So or Mrs. So and So and they type the paper. When will you have a paper ready for her to type?" Kemeny was asked. "I have three right here," he replied, causing most in the room to burst into laughter. But Professor B. H. Brown rolled his eyes and mumbled, "There are going to be some changes around here." Kemeny was ultimately given the power to hire whomever he wanted for the department. Kemeny would also encourage talented high school students to apply to Dartmouth as if he were a coach recruiting athletes for the football team.

At 43, Kemeny rose to the presidency of Dartmouth. As the institution's thirteenth president, just as he had been as department chairman, Kemeny was always well prepared and had his "ducks in order," according to colleague Thomas Kurtz. Kemeny instituted many changes at the college during his tenure as president. In 1972, Dartmouth admitted women students for the first time; the board of trustee's public vote was unanimous in favor of coeducation, although there was privately a bit of dissention: trustee David Parkhurst Smith later told Kemeny, "John, when coeducation came up, I opposed it. I was wrong." Kemeny revamped academic schedules, instituting a year-round trimester model. He retired the school's unofficial but offensive Indian mascot, supported civil rights initiatives, and actively recruited Native American and other minority students to campus. In 1979, President Carter tapped him to lead the investigation into the Three Mile Island reactor meltdown; the Kemeny Commission pulled no punches in its criticism of nuclear power procedures. In his last public address as president, Kemeny warned the study body of the growing intolerance and prejudice that was gaining a foothold in civilized society. Although he had continued to teach classes at Dartmouth during his presidency as well as perform periodic probability research with Professor J. Laurie Snell, in 1981 Kemeny retired as president and returned to teaching full-time until he passed away in 1992. Throughout his Dartmouth career, Kemeny, though slightly aloof, was warm, kind, open-minded and open to answer the questions of anyone who approached him, and especially disdained elitism; Kemeny had observed these same qualities in Einstein and von Neumann, and had decided to model himself after them.

As a young assistant professor at Princeton, Kemeny met his future wife, Jean Alexander, a self-described "Yankee from Maine" who was then a freshman at Smith College, at a Princeton World Federalist Conference. They married in 1950 and had two children, Jennifer and Robert, who both graduated from Dartmouth. Jean helped her husband manage affairs of state during his presidency; Kemeny noted that his Dartmouth presidency was a "two-person team effort."

In 1956, John Kemeny hired Thomas Kurtz to teach mathematics and statistics at Dartmouth. He had a signature look: a mop of dark hair and large dark frame glasses, capped off with a thick mustache. (Kemeny wore a small mustache but couldn't ever shake his thick Hungarian accent.) Kurtz's journey to Dartmouth wasn't nearly as eventful as Kemeny's. Kurtz was born on February 22, 1928, in Oak Park, Illinois. He graduated from the private liberal arts Knox College in Galesburg, Illinois, in 1950. From there it was on to Princeton for doctoral work; Kurtz's thesis advisor was John Tukey, arguably the greatest statistician of the twentieth century who was already something of a legend—with his prodigious mathematical output, his dual role as Princeton professor and Bell Labs researcher, and his coining of neologisms to describe new ideas.

Kurtz wrote his first computer program in 1951 as a graduate student at Princeton; although he ultimately received a degree in statistics, he had a strong interest in the nascent field of computing. Interestingly, as a Princeton grad student, he only lived about a block away from the Kemenys, although he didn't know them personally. In March of 1956, the year he completed his Ph.D., Kurtz made an appointment to interview with Kemeny, who had begun his mission to reshape the Dartmouth mathematics department by recruiting top young mathematicians. Kurtz was hired, but he was Kemeny's second choice; David Wallace, who turned down Dartmouth for the University of Chicago, was his first choice. Regardless, Kurtz, who loved the New England area, thinking it "gorgeous," accepted Kemeny's offer to come to Dartmouth which, unlike Kurtz's undergraduate alma matter, was not yet a coeducational institution.

When Kurtz first arrived at the mathematics department, located on the top floor of Dartmouth Hall, he worked almost exclusively with Kemeny. There were roughly a dozen members of the math department then, which included two professors of astronomy as well. (Eventually, astronomy merged with the physics department.) At faculty meetings and departmental parties (which were often held in cramped apartments), Kemeny regaled the assembled faculty with personal stories from his well-traveled life. Kurtz was struck by Kemeny's intellectually "eclectic views," realizing that Kemeny had many varied interests in mathematics and logic and the philosophy of science but didn't seem married to any subspecialty of mathematics.

Early on, money was tight for Kurtz. When Kemeny hired him, Kurtz's wife Agnes said, "This is not enough money." Kurtz had taken a pay cut from his graduate student days to join the Dartmouth faculty, and he didn't know what he was going to do with his statistics expertise—teaching seemed as good an option as any at the time. But there was a solution to Kurtz's salary gap that Kemeny suggested: IBM was promoting computing on college campuses like the Massachusetts Institute of Technology (MIT). The IBM system used batch processing, and, as part of the deal, some academic institutions in New England would receive computer time as well. Dartmouth assistant professor of mathematics John McCarthy, who coined the term artificial intelligence, contacted MIT and designated Kurtz as the liaison between the MIT machines and Dartmouth. (McCarthy would shortly thereafter join the MIT faculty, granting him ready access to computers on campus; he would later create the programming language LISP.) As such, Kurtz was to promote at Dartmouth the uses and power of the computing system at MIT; Kurtz would also be responsible for carrying a steel box containing punch cards written in SAP (the IBM SHARE Symbolic Assembly Program) from Dartmouth to MIT's campus every two weeks. He would catch the 6:20 AM train out of White River Junction, arrive at Boston around three hours later, and then have a cab take him to MIT. Kurtz inserted the punch cards into the IBM 704's input hopper at MIT's computer center in Building 26, waiting patiently for hours until printouts emerged. Kurtz then packed up these printouts to take back to Dartmouth.

It's the way things were back then—computers were ungainly and expensive and thus required specialized operators to take care of the details. Jobs were fed into computers in batches, which took hours or perhaps as long as a day to complete. Hence the term "batch processing." Which might have been fine, Kurtz later reflected, if the programs worked; instead, after waiting all that time, users frequently got error reports back on their printouts, leaving these users back at square one. In fact, Kurtz himself took a month to realize that a program he thought he wrote perfectly in SAP in fact didn't work at all, simply because the turnaround time between jobs had been so long.

There had to be an easier way.

CHAPTER 3

∞

The Birth of Time-Sharing

John Kemeny loved shrimp, football, science fiction, and Agatha Christie mysteries, but he hated, absolutely hated, batch processing.

Kemeny had first encountered the difficulties of batch processing when he consulted for the RAND Corporation back in 1956. It wasn't only the frequent error messages on printouts that bothered him, though. Sometimes, nothing would print out at all; other times, cards jammed the machine. Worse yet, he would witness mathematicians wasting their time standing in line for hours to get no more than mere seconds at the machine. Before he left, Kemeny recommended that the batch system be altered to permit interruptions, a suggestion never taken up because such interruptions were incompatible with batch processing.

By the late 1950s, Kemeny decided to purchase a computer for Dartmouth. This would not be Dartmouth's first foray into computer technology, though. In 1940, well before Kemeny and Kurtz arrived at the college, Bell Labs mathematician George Stibitz—who had several years earlier built the Complex Number Computer, which performed mathematical computations using relays—operated a relay computer from a terminal at a remote location: Stibitz, along with a contingent of mathematicians, was at McNutt Hall at Dartmouth for an American Mathematical Society meeting, while the computer doing the work was in New York City. The machine took about twenty seconds to report back the result of a multiplication problem—considered a "lightning-like speed" at the time. It was the first public demonstration of the remote operation of a computer.

Kemeny and Kurtz shopped around for a computer, ultimately settling on a popular desk computer: the drum-based, sixteen-instruction LGP-30 (Librascope General Precision), a product of the Librascope company. Don Morrison, then the provost, controlled Dartmouth's purse strings. Shortly before Morrison died, Kemeny walked down to his office and said, "We need $40,000 for this beast." (The LGP-30 ended up costing about $37,000.) But there was no budget for the machine, because money was tied up in constructing the new Bradley mathematics building, named in honor of a famous alumnus of Dartmouth (Albert Bradley). But the fund for the building did include provisions for "Furniture and Decorations." So, the LDP-30 was no longer a computer—it was furniture. And the money was now made available.

In 1959, Kurtz, Kemeny, and their wives all traveled together in a station wagon to pick up the computer from the Royal McBee Corporation. The Bradley building was still a couple years away from completion, so they stored the relatively small LGP-30 in the basement of College Hall, once occupied by the college's resident photographer. That summer, Kemeny had Honors Program undergraduates—there were no graduate students at Dartmouth—work with the computer. For instance, physics major Robert Hargraves, one of those Honors students, wrote a FORTRAN-like language and compiler called DART for the LGP-30 in only a few weeks. When the computer was finally relocated to the new Bradley building, undergraduates Hargraves, Steve Garland, Jorge Llacer, and Anthony Knapp pooled their resources to write an ALGOL 60 compiler for the machine. ALGOL was a popular and respected computer language then, and the undergrads had a primer of language features to work off of. LGP-30 ALGOL programs were written on paper tape, but the compiler was set up in such a way that as many as five students could run their programs in only a quarter of an hour; they called the process SCALP (the Self-Contained ALGOL Processor): it was still batch processing, but streamlined. Other students were using the machine to analyze poetry, search for prime numbers, and (correctly) predict Kennedy-Nixon New Hampshire presidential primary election results, letting the LGP-30 run through the night and retrieving the results the next morning. At professional share-group conferences for the LGP-30, which Kurtz and some Dartmouth students attended, the "experienced" older users of the LGP-30 were shocked at the uses that the Dartmouth undergrads were putting the little computer to; they had been content to use the machine for advanced tabulation, not high-level programming.

If the batch-processing problem could be solved, Kemeny and Kurtz, by this point, had ample proof that at least some Dartmouth undergraduates could and would make interesting use of computers. MIT and Bell Labs were experimenting with a new concept called time-sharing that would allow multiple users to work on the same computer nearly simultaneously. During a visit Kurtz had with John McCarthy at MIT, McCarthy suggested to him, "You guys ought to do time-sharing." McCarthy knew of what he spoke; by 1959, MIT had already devised a system whereby user terminals were hooked up to a computer (a Digital Equipment Corporation PDP-1), and the computer's operating system would cycle through the terminals, one by one, spending a small amount of time running programs submitted by each terminal until a particular user's job was completed. Small jobs wouldn't take forever, but larger jobs would take more time. It was a revolutionary—and much fairer—way to exploit a computer's resources.

When Kurtz returned from MIT, he sat Kemeny down and said, "Don't you think the time is approaching when every student should learn how to program a computer?" Kemeny replied, "Sure, Tom, but it isn't physically possible to teach so many students." Then Kurtz explained the time-sharing concept to Kemeny, noting that computer instruction might be possible for hundreds of students on campus. But not with their small LGP-30; although they had already demonstrated that multiple students could dispatch programs at a fairly rapid clip on the machine (with SCALP), still only one student at a time could make use of it. "Dartmouth had the largest open stack library in the world at that time in a college of this type and the concept of open stack computing, that was my idea," Kurtz reflected years later, adding, "That's one of the few ideas that I had that Kemeny didn't have." In the coming years, giving students this freedom would greatly enhance Dartmouth's reputation. Yet Dartmouth would first need to get ahold of a more powerful computer than the LGP-30 to satisfy Kurtz's vision.

Kemeny had a key role to play in bringing Kurtz's time-sharing vision to life: raise money for the hardware. He first went to the president of Dartmouth, John Sloan Dickey, as well as to the Board of Trustees. People such as Dean Leonard M. Rieser and the dean of the Thayer School of Engineering, Myron Tribus, were quickly sold on the time-sharing idea. In fact, Tribus had once been an executive at GE and still had connections to the company. Specifically, Tribus told Kemeny and Kurtz of a manager at the GE Process Computers site at Phoenix, Arizona—where Arnold Spielberg had worked—named Clair C. Lasher whom they might be able to do business with.

Following that lead, Kurtz called GE and told them of the time-sharing idea, bluntly asking the company, "Would you be interested in donating a computer?" GE invited a Dartmouth team to Phoenix. Tony Knapp, who had helped code ALGOL 60 for the LGP-30, wrote up a fifteen-page time-sharing proposal, replete with block diagrams, for GE brass to examine. Knapp, along with Kurtz, made the trip to Phoenix. During the long airplane ride, Knapp and Kurtz talked a great deal, fine-tuning their detailed proposal. But when they arrived, as Kurtz recalls, they were "treated as customers"—the Dartmouth team was taken to dinner and a show—with GE not particularly caring about the engineering logistics of the proposal. The Dartmouth team flew back to New Hampshire, seemingly empty-handed. But a few people at GE had recognized the value of the time-sharing idea; these few managed to work out a deal with Dartmouth. Like at IBM, where computers were offered to high-profile firms or educational institutions at a discount as a marketing ploy, GE agreed to set a 60 percent discount on their computers. (Other companies, such IBM and National Cash, had also responded to Dartmouth's proposal to purchase computers for a time-sharing setup, but GE offered the college the best deal.) Now Kemeny needed to figure out how to pay for the hardware.

Kemeny wrote up a National Science Foundation (NSF) grant, and spoke to the trustees. The NSF grant was for the equipment (which ran into the hundreds of thousands of dollars), while the trustees offered to cover the lease-purchase agreement. The NSF, however, initially balked at the proposal. The reviewers thought that Dartmouth was understaffed and in over their heads. How could so few faculty members, coupled with a handful of undergraduates who would program the system, build and maintain a cutting-edge time-sharing complex?

Yet despite the negative reviews and the reluctance to part with money for a proposal with such a seemingly shaky foundation, Kemeny's glad-handing and persuasive personal style—he knew quite a few people at the NSF—landed Dartmouth a good portion of the requested funds, enough to purchase the hardware outright, which included not only the GE-225 but also the GE DATANET-30. Kemeny had drummed up excitement at the NSF for time-sharing, leveraging a mass of Dartmouth's undergrads in order to bring significant computing power to the college—thereby creating the Dartmouth Time-Sharing System (DTSS) in 1964, rather than having to rely on another university's computer system (like MIT's) or in-house batch processing on a computer of modest power, like the LGP-30. Two undergrads were especially vital to setting up DTSS: John McGeachie and Mike Busch. With no manuals or printed technical specs available, they figured out how to have the two different GE computers on campus communicate with each other, something the machines were never designed to do. In fact, McGeachie and Busch began writing the DTSS operating system *before* Dartmouth ever received the computers. (One machine, the "slave" GE-225, was assigned the calculations, while the other machine, the "master" GE DATANET-30, was tasked with commutating with the terminals. After the DTSS gained traction, GE packaged the two computers as one: the GE-265, which came with the Dartmouth time-sharing software already installed.) Dartmouth also hired a computer hardware maintenance man from GE to service the two machines full-time for a couple of years, keeping the hardware—which wasn't especially reliable—in check. Despite any hardware hiccups, the undergrads were always there and always busy, day and night, pecking away at the machines, programming the future.

Interestingly, IBM was not happy that Dartmouth had gone with GE. Several IBM representatives visited Dartmouth behind the backs of Kemeny and Kurtz. The IBM reps went directly to the provost, arguing that "Kemeny's folks don't know what they are doing." But the provost kicked them out. Big Blue was very much a bully in those days, trying to ensure that their machines were purchased over their competitors'. "I think Bill Gates learned most of his lessons from IBM," Kurtz humorously posited. (Eventually,

IBM gained a foothold at Dartmouth, only in the end to be supplanted by the Apple Macintosh with its superior networking capabilities.)

Yet over time, the relationship between Dartmouth and GE frayed. Early on, GE marketed and sold time-sharing services that were identical to Dartmouth's. GE even hired Dartmouth undergrads to maintain their systems during school breaks. One summer, however, one such student hacked into a supposedly "secure" time-sharing terminal and had it print a message containing oblique references to Dartmouth and GE right in the middle of an inspection tour by GE brass. The message read, "The Jolly Green Giant strides through the Valley of the Giants!"

Several years later, Dartmouth helped GE launch a new time-sharing system based off of the GE-635. Dartmouth wrote a new BASIC compiler for the system; GE wrote the operating system for the machine, calling it Phase 1. By the early 1970s, Dartmouth president John Dickey had resigned due to a controversy over the ROTC on campus, the trustees installed Kemeny as his replacement, and Dartmouth and GE parted ways, with GE ending up with the world's largest time-sharing business (and a profitable business at that), along with a later version of Dartmouth BASIC (the fifth such implementation) that would never be updated or improved at Dartmouth but would nevertheless be indiscriminately copied and modified by others—setting the stage for many of the problems to come.

CHAPTER 4

∞

The Creation of BASIC

In John Kemeny's mad dash to put his stamp on the Dartmouth mathematics department, he effectively used the school's undergraduates as currency with the NSF to procure some of the most advanced computing hardware in the world at the time—and then leaned on those same undergraduates (who were more than happy to oblige, interested as they were in exploiting the hardware), along with his direct report, Thomas Kurtz, to help build a time-sharing system and create the programming language that would popularize it: not ALGOL or FORTRAN, as the technocratic bourgeoisie might have anticipated, but a general-purpose language for the proletariat: BASIC, the Beginner's All-purpose Symbolic Instruction Code.

Kemeny proposed to Kurtz that they write a new language for DTSS; yet it wouldn't be their first crack at creating a new computer language. In 1956, they had programmed Darsimco (Dartmouth Simplified Code), designed to shortcut some of the tedium required when coding in the assembly language SAP for the IBM 704. Their colleagues, however, failed to use it. There was also DOPE (Dartmouth Oversimplified Programming Experiment) for the LGP-30 that then-high school student Sidney Marshall wrote with Kemeny while taking calculus on campus; DOPE, however, was too limited.

"Surely we can do better than FORTRAN for teaching purposes?" Kemeny rhetorically asked Kurtz, but Kurtz didn't initially believe that they could do better. What if no one adopted the language we make? Kurtz thought. Kurtz figured that they could instead teach undergraduates programming on the DTSS using some of the easier subsets of ALGOL or FORTRAN, essentially simplifying huge swaths of an established language. But that approach quickly proved to be a nonstarter: no matter how much of ALGOL Kurtz stripped away, he was still left with quirky punctuation rules—but dispose of the syntax, and he'd be left with an entirely different language altogether. And FORTRAN was no better, saddled with a series of syntactical elements that were esoteric at best, frustratingly misguided at worst (famously, FORTRAN is so picky that a single typo in a program resulted in the unintentional destruction of the Venus-bound NASA Mariner 1 spacecraft, although this story may be apocryphal); nonetheless, removing these elements, as with ALGOL, fundamentally changed the language. Perhaps instead of culling a subset of ALGOL or FORTRAN, there was a language simple enough for teaching purposes. Kurtz stumbled upon JOSS (JOHNNIAC Open Shop System), a time-sharing system language built for the JOHNNIAC computer at RAND. But JOSS, too, had an unnatural syntax; for instance, decimal points weren't permitted with numbers.

If Kemeny and Kurtz really were going to make programming accessible to all undergrads, then they had to write something user-friendly. Kemeny was so focused on user-friendliness that he had pushed for using the words **HELLO** and **GOODBYE** in place of **LOGON** and **LOGOFF** on the DTSS. Kurtz was finally in agreement with Kemeny that a new language was the only viable solution. In building this new language, they would borrow some of the best features of established languages—such as subscripted variables and the **GOTO** statement from FORTRAN, and loop structures from ALGOL (FORTRAN's loop syntax wasn't particularly intuitive)—but rethink them, putting a premium on ease-of-use, consistency, and understandability, especially for the layperson. "Why should a new user be forced to learn a complex language just to communicate with the computer?" Kemeny asked, continuing, "Why not teach the computer a language it can understand and at the same time is easy for human beings to learn and use?"

For instance, Kemeny insisted that all statements in BASIC *must* begin with an English word so the user knows precisely what operation is supposed to occur on each line. Other languages didn't have this requirement. For example, ALGOL and FORTRAN used assignment operators in statements that could just as easily pass for algebraic equations. Take this line:

> T=X+1

But the statement cannot be rearranged, as you might by using algebra, into this:

> X=T-1

Instead, **T=X+1** is a statement of *variable assignment*, meaning that the variable to the left of the equals sign—the **T**—has its value set equal to the value of the variable **X** plus one unit. Thus, a statement like the following—which would be valid algebraically—is not a valid statement of variable assignment in either FORTRAN or ALGOL:

> 1=T-X

Kemeny wanted an explicit keyword to designate variable assignment, so he chose **LET**. In BASIC, instead of **T=X+1**, the statement would read

> LET T=X+1

which, to Kemeny's ear, sounded more like a prototypical mathematician "letting" some variable equal something else and thus was a logical choice. (In later, non-Dartmouth implementations of BASIC, **LET** became optional, thus damaging Kemeny and Kurtz's structure of a single BASIC statement starting every line. In addition, to save memory in early microcomputer implementations programmers were allowed to concatenate multiple BASIC statements into one line, also antithetical to Kemeny and Kurtz's vision.)

There were a total of fourteen statements in the first implementation of Dartmouth BASIC. All were English words, purposely chosen (or swiped from FORTRAN or ALGOL) to be as easy to remember as possible. Besides **LET**, there was

- **DATA**, for storing immutable data ("immutable" here means unchangeable during runtime; the data for **DATA** had to be hardcoded into the program itself);
- **DEF**, for function definition;
- **DIM**, for dimensioning an array (a group of variables, systematically indexed);
- **END**, a required keyword signaling the end of the program (the appearance of **END** alerted users that they had reached a program's final line);
- **FOR/TO/STEP**, describing the layout of a loop (i.e., cycle through the loop from number x to number y, going by z's);
- **GOSUB**, an unconditional jump from the main program to a subroutine; transfers control of the program to the first statement of the subroutine; analogous to the call instruction of assembly code;
- **GOTO**, an unconditional jump to a statement at a specified line number; analogous to the jump instruction of assembly code;
- **IF/THEN**, a control structure for decision-making; if a particular condition is true, then perform some action (e.g., unconditionally jump);
- **NEXT**, specifying the end of loops;
- **PRINT**, for outputting characters, either on the teletypewriter or a display monitor;
- **READ**, for reading in immutable data (courtesy of the **DATA** statement) and storing this data into variables;
- **REM**, a remark or comment (i.e., characters that are ignored by the compiler, which serve as notes to the programmer);
- **RETURN**, returns control back to the main program from a subroutine; analogous to the return instruction of assembly code;
- **STOP**, halts a program; functionally the same as the **END** statement but not required.

Arithmetic operations included addition (+), subtraction (-), multiplication (*), division (/), and raising to a power (^). There were also operating system commands such as **HELLO**, to start a new user session; **NEW**, to start a new program; **OLD**, to load a program; **LIST**, to output the code of the program loaded in memory; **SAVE**, to store the program in nonvolatile memory; **CATALOG**, to see a list of the programs in nonvolatile memory; **RUN**, to execute the program loaded in memory; and **BYE** or **GOODBYE**, to end the user session. The user interacted with the DTSS using a command-line interface.

Based on Kemeny and Kurtz's designs for BASIC, Kemeny began writing the first BASIC compiler—which translated BASIC programs into machine code—on punch cards in 1963, well before the DTSS was in place; meanwhile, Kurtz oversaw the students who were working on the DTSS. Kemeny, who had never written a compiler before, needed to test his BASIC compiler on GE hardware, which hadn't arrived at Dartmouth yet. So that summer Kemeny hired William M. "Bill" Zani, out of the Tuck School of Business, to help him as an assistant (Zani had a GE connection: his brother was a salesman for the company); Kemeny would present Zani handwritten notes every morning, going over the code with Zani, and then Zani was tasked with transcribing the notes into punch cards. It was hard work, for both of them. There were thousands of lines of code. Parts of Kemeny's handwritten compiler worked, but parts of it did not. (And Kemeny admits that as much debugging as he and Zani did—they were forced to debug the compiler with a GE computer in Boston—there were still several errors in the first implementation of BASIC, namely, incorrect calculations of some squares and issues with the **INT**, or integer, function.) Some programs initially worked as anticipated; in fact, Zani claims that he was the first person to ever actually see a BASIC program run. Remember that Zani worked for Kemeny in the summer of 1963, well before the soon-to-be-famous May 1, 1964, date of the birth of BASIC; however, even Kurtz labels this birthdate a "pretty good myth" because neither he nor Kemeny was on-site and there are no pictures memorializing the event. Regardless, on the night of May 1, 1964, at around 4:00 AM, undergrads John McGeachie and Mike Busch finally had the DTSS operating system working and successfully ran slightly different BASIC programs simultaneously on separate teletypewriters. One of those first programs, producing an output of **5**, read as follows:

```
10 LET X=(7+8)/3
20 PRINT X
30 END
```

The single-pass BASIC compiler worked; the time-sharing system worked. And "the infants birth-cries, of course, were in BASIC!" Kemeny wrote enthusiastically. (Interestingly, despite Kurtz's later accusation of myth-making, Kemeny and Kurtz's own book from 1985 titled *Back to BASIC* states that it wasn't McGeachie and Busch operating the terminals that May the First morning but that "…John Kemeny and a student programmer were sitting at neighboring terminals and typing programs in BASIC. They typed RUN at the same time and were deliriously happy when both got correct answers." Yet in the Dartmouth-produced documentary *The Birth of BASIC*, released on the fiftieth anniversary of the language's birth, only McGeachie and Busch are mentioned as stationed at terminals and running BASIC programs that night; Kemeny is nowhere to be found.)

Kemeny and Kurtz were very deliberate and methodical when they put BASIC together. As little as possible was left to chance; they would argue over each step, making sure the best choices were made at every turn. They designed the language together, laying out features that BASIC had to have, including that the language be general-purpose and easy to use, give understandable error messages, keep the user insulated from the hardware and operating system, and be able to run small programs quickly: the user shouldn't have to individually compile, then link, then load, and then execute a program—rather, all these steps should be taken care of automatically behind the scenes whenever a BASIC program is run by the compiler. To keep things accessible for the beginner, they decreed that each line of BASIC contain only a single instruction; unlike in JOSS or ALGOL, program statements didn't need to be ended by using punctuation like semicolons. Arithmetic was performed entirely in floating point (decimals) so users didn't ever have to explicitly specify between numeric types (e.g., integer or floating point); the GE computers had floating-point arithmetic hardware already built-in. As new BASIC features were added later by student programmers, Kemeny and Kurtz made sure that these "advanced features" stayed out of sight, accessible only when the user was ready for them. BASIC would select the easiest "default options," making choices for the beginner—for example with the output format of numbers—leaving the messy details behinds the scenes; the more expert user could fiddle with those default options at his leisure, changing them to suit his needs. "Once you have learned to program, new computer languages are easy to learn," Kurtz reflected years later. "The first is the hardest.... The simpler the first language, the more easily the average student will learn it."

Starting statements with line numbers—students were encouraged to number lines by tens, leaving room in between just in case lines needed to be inserted later—permitted interactivity but was in fact a legacy feature of punched cards, where line numbers allowed a user to correctly sort the cards of a lengthy program if they somehow became unsorted. FORTRAN also used statement (i.e., line) numbers but only as addresses for control transfer statements (e.g., conditional jumps, which were implemented, as in BASIC, by using **IF** statements); most lines in FORTRAN, therefore, didn't require numbering.

In BASIC, if the user needed to fix one line, he did not have to retype the whole program—only the line. From the first implementation of BASIC, typing a single line number without any statement on the line indicated that the user wished to delete the entire line from the program. Inserting spaces didn't matter—BASIC was space-independent, ignoring spaces between tokens (i.e., characters of the source code), so that users, especially faculty members who perhaps weren't particularly adept at using the Teletype's QWERTY keyboard (Kemeny wasn't a nimble typist), had a margin for (typing) error. But space independence was likely another idea lifted from FORTRAN. John Backus, whose IBM group developed FORTRAN, traced the origins of the practice to an issue known to IBM 704 SHARE users' association members: that of keypunchers miscounting blanks. Backus also felt that a programmer should be able to style his program in a cogent and readable form, and a FORTRAN compiler that ignored blanks would further that aim.

In BASIC, error messages, which would not be allowed to overwhelm the user, would refer to the line number containing the error. (Some example error messages: **DIMENSION TOO LARGE, ILLEGAL LINE NUMBER, ILLEGAL FORMULA**—"[p]erhaps the most common error message," according to the first Dartmouth BASIC manual—and **FOR WITHOUT NEXT**.) The compiler would report at most five errors. Furthermore, unlike later implementations of BASIC, which were usually interpreters, compiled BASIC wouldn't run a program containing syntax errors. (All Dartmouth BASIC implementations were compilers; BASIC interpreters require much less memory and computational power than compilers and thus became the standard on the early underpowered microcomputers.)

By the third Dartmouth BASIC implementation, the **INPUT** statement was added. **INPUT** paused the program, waiting on the user to supply some information. **INPUT** turned BASIC programs from advanced calculators into interactive coaches and game opponents; without **INPUT**, there are no BASIC games, and interest in the language would probably have waned quickly. Such interactivity, a feature that Kemeny and Kurtz weren't initially sold on, was only possible thanks to the time-sharing system, which ran only a small portion of each user's program at a time. It had taken several years to add **INPUT** because the statement paused one of the two GE time-sharing computers; a "swap" to disk was devised to permit the system to continue running other users' programs. But it was time well spent: the user-friendliness of BASIC's **INPUT** and **PRINT** statements stood in stark contrast to the complexities of FORTRAN's I/O statements, which required the programmer to specify formatting rules in advance.

In 1966, the DTSS moved to the Kiewit Computation Center in the newly constructed Kiewit Building. The building was named in honor of a millionaire donor who attended Dartmouth for a short time: Peter Kiewit. It was his wife, Evelyn, who helped convince her husband to part with the money to build the modern, computer-centric facilities. The GE computers' location at College Hall had become unsustainable due to the increased demand for DTSS access. Kemeny penned a brochure introducing the Kiewit Computation Center to Dartmouth students, which enumerated the many advantages of the time-sharing setup. (Strangely, the brochure calls BASIC the "Beginners' All-purpose Simplified Instruction Code," rather than "Symbolic.") At Kiewit, the hardware was situated in a large room with glass walls; a retired marine sergeant named Henry Robert Schramm, who had served in Okinawa, was hired as the first machine room operator for the new GE-635, with its 160K of "core storage" memory as well as 768K of "drum storage." The

BASIC compiler occupied about 5K of the core storage. ("K" refers to a kilobyte, which is 2^{10}, or 1024, bytes.)

"With a time-sharing computer, when I have a problem to solve on the machine, I can sit down at a teletype console and have the computer available to me until I am finished," Kemeny wrote, despite the scores of simultaneous users on campus as well as teletypewriters in dozens of other colleges and high schools tapping into the DTSS, including at Hanover High School (of which Kemeny served on the school board) and Phillips Exeter Academy. Dan Rockmore, then a high school student and later a professor of mathematics and computer science at Dartmouth (he would ultimately become the John G. Kemeny Parents Professor of Mathematics, an endowed professorship established in 1981), remembers his first experience with BASIC: "I was in Mr. Bullman's class in Metuchen High School and I'm almost sure that I wrote a program to play poker." The phone company had to install new trunk lines to keep up with the demand on the DTSS, despite Dartmouth's phone lines' optimization using frequency division multiplexing. "As a result, each user of our computer has the illusion that the machine is there just to serve him and that he has complete control of the entire system," Kemeny explained.

Furthermore, computer use was entirely free: Kurtz compared the open-access system to an "open stack library," refusing to put up barriers to use like monetary charges or written permission; "computing [like the library] was a fixed cost—it cost the same whether it was used or not—so why not let the students use it?" Kurtz asked rhetorically. In a post-presidency interview, Kemeny gave the lion's share of credit to Kurtz for convincing the trustees to view the computing center as they viewed the library: after all, you wouldn't charge students for taking books out from the library. Kemeny pointedly calls this computer-library connection Kurtz's "greatest contribution." Thus, the inauguration of the revolutionary DTSS arguably also spelled the beginning of the personal computer revolution.

And just as Dartmouth didn't attempt to leverage the DTSS for commercial gain, the BASIC programming language was not copyrighted, trademarked, or patented; such legal protections might have prevented BASIC's spread and implementation on time-sharing networks and thus be counterproductive to Kemeny and Kurtz's mission of computing being available for all students.

When people asked Kemeny and Kurtz if they were allowed to copy the language, they replied, "Fine." When IBM asked them if they could rewrite BASIC for one of their time-sharing systems, Kemeny and Kurtz again replied, "Fine. All you have to do is give us credit in the front of your manual." Even before Microsoft began selling BASIC interpreters, Kurtz estimates that around five million people worldwide were exposed to BASIC programming. That wouldn't have happened without BASIC being released into the public domain.

Of course, the locus of most of that exposure came at Dartmouth. Dozens of Dartmouth students were able to work on the DTSS simultaneously. At first, Kemeny encouraged his staff to include a BASIC programming component in every mathematics class. BASIC then became a mandatory part of all freshman mathematics classes (Kurtz later noted that only about an hour was required to teach freshman students how to write simple programs in BASIC). More and more terminals were added on campus. Within a few years, the vast majority of Dartmouth undergraduates (perhaps as high as 85 percent, which rocketed to over 90 percent by the early 1970s), in math, science, sociology and the social sciences, and even art and music courses, were using the DTSS; nearly half of the faculty made use of the DTSS, too, although Kemeny encountered some pushback: in an post-presidency interview, he said that some mathematics faculty members told him that they've "taught [their courses] well for 25 years and see no reason why [they] should make dramatic changes in it.... Some of my best friends [among the faculty] fit that description." Kemeny added that "underlying their [these faculty members'] arrogance may be fear.... They hate to admit it that they don't know how to use a computer." To handle these resisters, Kemeny suggested converting a small group of enthusiastic faculty to the benefits of computer use and then "let[ing] them be the missionaries."

Regardless, Kemeny and Kurtz had seen their vision become a reality: every student on campus had access to a computer, and every faculty member had access to a computer for classroom purposes. Dartmouth was a liberal arts campus that had fallen under the spell of computing. When it came to programming in BASIC, the first Dartmouth BASIC manual offered a key piece of advice taken from the mathematician Richard Hamming: Typing is no substitute for thinking.

Dartmouth students were also fashioning interactive BASIC games to play—not as part of their coursework, but purely for entertainment. Kemeny ultimately was supportive of BASIC being used recreationally. One of the most popular BASIC games on campus was in fact written by Kemeny: called *Dartmouth Championship Football*, it was a text-based videogame (all games were text-only in those early days; no BASIC graphics commands existed for teletypewriters which, regardless, printed at slow speeds of around ten to fifteen characters per second) that pitted Dartmouth against rival Princeton, which was controlled by the computer. There were tackles, touchdowns, fumbles, interceptions, and field goals, and a user's decisions affected the outcome of the game. More than just the **INPUT** statement was required for the football simulation. The **RND** function, only one of a set of extensive built-in mathematical functions (others included **ABS**, for absolute values; **LOG**, for logarithms; **SQR**, for square roots; **INT**, for the integer portion of numbers; and a set of trigonometric functions taking angle measures in radians), produced "random" floating-point numbers between 0 and 1. The numbers weren't truly random—hence the scare quotes in the previous sentence—but pseudorandom, generated according to a deterministic mathematical function. **RND** took a "dummy argument," meaning that the character or number inside the parentheses of the function was ignored by the compiler; for instance, **RND(5)** would still produce a random number between 0 and 1, not between 0 and 5.

Take a look at some of the first handful of BASIC lines from *Dartmouth Championship Football*:

```
0 REM    *   FTBALL   *
...
50 LET T=0
60 LET S(0)=0
70 LET S(2)=0
100 PRINT "TOSS OF COIN. (TYPE A NO. FROM 1
    TO 300)";
120 INPUT Z1
140 FOR I=1 TO Z1
160 LET X=RND(X)
180 NEXT I
190 IF RND(Z)>1/2 THEN 195
191 PRINT "PRINCETON WON THE TOSS"
```

```
193 GOTO 2180
195 PRINT "DARTMOUTH WON THE TOSS"
```

Line **0** is a remark, or comment, ignored by the compiler. Line **50** initializes the value of a new variable, **T**, to **0** (the line has an opcode, **LET**, and two addresses, the **T** and the **0**; most BASIC lines follow that form), while lines **60** and **70** create an array variable, called **S**, and initialize two of **S**'s elements to **0**. A **PRINT** statement outputs user instructions on line **100**. Line **120** gathers input from the user—specifically, an integer from **1** to **300**—and stores this input into a variable called **Z1**. This is effectively a user-generated random seed value, utilized in order to run a loop **Z1** times (see lines **140** to **180**) in order to land on a (hopefully surprising) number, between 0 and 1, that the **RND** function returns. Line **190** contains a conditional statement: if the **RND** value is greater than ½, then Dartmouth won the coin toss; otherwise, Princeton won the coin toss. The game continues in kind from there.

Kemeny and Kurtz never made it their business to investigate what the students were up to on the DTSS; after all, as Kemeny wrote, "[A]ny student may walk into the Kiewit Computation Center, sit down at a console, and use the time-sharing system. No one will ask if he is solving a serious research problem, doing his homework the easy way, playing a game of football, or writing a letter to his girlfriend." Dartmouth students even wrote a BASIC dating application, an ancestor to modern dating apps.

The democratization of computing, and not just at Dartmouth, was underway, thanks to the two-pronged effort of time-sharing and the implementation of an accessible programming language, BASIC, that ran on the system. Kemeny was so proud of his digital creation that he ordered a vanity license plate for his convertible that read only a single word: BASIC.

CHAPTER 5

∞

Many Changes, Many BASICs

After the first implementation of Dartmouth BASIC, Kemeny, Kurtz, and the undergraduates most closely tied to time-sharing worked to improve the language. But as new versions of BASIC emerged from Dartmouth, older versions found their way outside of the DTSS and began to proliferate and mutate.

The first Dartmouth BASIC implementation, which Kemeny and Kurtz called BASIC the First, was released in 1964. It was limited; there was no **INPUT** statement, for instance (that would arrive by the third implementation), the **DEF** statement permitted only the simplest of function definitions and names (**FNA** to **FNZ**, or 26 possibilities), and string variables and constants weren't possible at first. Even numeric variable names had to be simple: a single letter like **N**, or a letter and a number, like **Z1**; this allowed for 286—that is, 26+26×10—potential variable names. (Things were kept simple so that the single-pass BASIC compiler would work smoothly.) Even the **PRINT** statement, which output characters to the terminal, was barebones, only allowing for commas to separate discrete blocks of characters in fifteen-character-wide "print zones," like this:

```
10 LET Y=10
20 PRINT "TEN IS: ", Y
30 END
```

```
RUN

TEN IS:                 10
```

Soon thereafter, the semicolon option was added so that output could be "packed" together:

```
10 LET Y=10
20 PRINT "TEN IS: "; Y
30 END

RUN

TEN IS: 10
```

By the sixth implementation of BASIC, or BASIC the Sixth, the **PRINT** statement was given a counterpart: the **PRINT USING** statement, which permitted complex formatting of output (e.g., numerical amounts displayed in dollars). The **INPUT** statement, by this point, had also obtained a counterpart: **LINPUT** (which later became **LINE INPUT**), allowing for any character or characters—not just numbers—to be entered as input by the user during runtime. In addition, BASIC was also jury-rigged to handle the importation of items like text files.

Arrays caused Kemeny and Kurtz the most consternation. BASIC the First defaulted to a lower bound subscript of 1, not 0; thus, arrays were not zero-indexed. Soon enough, however, the zeroth element was added by default. Without using the **DIM** statement to declare a one- or two-dimensional array (which were the only two options), instead simply initializing array elements with no declaration—as seen in the program listing of *Dartmouth Championship Football* on lines **60** and **70**—the array would automatically be granted eleven elements with the subscripts 0, 1, 2, …, 10. Use the **DIM** statement to declare the array, and the user would have access to more elements (albeit always one more than was asked for, thanks to the default zeroth element). Tied to arrays were matrices, which were in effect two-dimensional arrays. The **MAT** statement operated on these two-dimensional arrays with ease, but there were discrepancies because **MAT** wasn't zero-indexed—it operated like the first version of the **DIM** statement, with lower bound subscripts of 1.

Early on, Kemeny and Kurtz knew that BASIC had to allow users the ability to store and manipulate strings. But they needed some way to differentiate between variables that stored numerical data and those that stored string data. Failing to locate many free keys on the Teletype, they resorted to the dollar sign (**$**) to mark the difference: "Then one of us observed that $ looks like *S* for *string*, and the convention was adopted. Had we known how many millions would end up using 'name$' and 'word$' in BASIC, we might have given more thought to the choice!" Strings were converted by the compiler, character by character, into ASCII codes (American Standard Code for Information Interchange, a series of numbers that correspond with printed characters) that could then be worked with arithmetically. Dartmouth BASIC users would eventually be given convenient options for manipulating strings, like concatenation (joining strings together), capturing substrings (with the **SEG$** function, which returns a designated substring), and finding the length of strings (with the **LEN** function, which returns a number, not a string—hence, no dollar sign in its name). But just when it looked like all the issues with Dartmouth BASIC had finally been sorted out with 1970's BASIC the Sixth, the roof began to leak.

Kemeny and Kurtz laid out three significant challenges in *Back to BASIC* that BASIC faced in the 1970s: first, the advent of "plotting," an antecedent of the graphical capabilities of personal computers; second, the emergence of structured programming; and third, the standardization of the BASIC language.

"Plotting" allowed for users to interact graphically with programs. A professor at Dartmouth, Arthur Luehrmann, wrote a library of BASIC graphics subroutines, easily imported, that gave BASIC programmers access to plotting capabilities; then Luehrmann consolidated the library, adapting the BASIC language itself to allow for graphics statements such as **PLOT**. Interest was so high in the graphics capabilities of BASIC that in 1974 a "Working Conference on Graphics in BASIC" was convened at the Minary Conference Center at Squam Lake that brought together experts from the business and education worlds.

The emergence of structured programming, the second challenge that BASIC encountered in the 1970s, is covered in chapter 14. Needless to say, Dartmouth Professor Stephen Garland, who as an undergraduate had helped to write ALGOL for Dartmouth's LGP-30, developed a structured version of BASIC the Sixth called SBASIC (Structured BASIC). SBASIC added new loop structures, an optional **ELSE** statement—for more advanced conditionals—as well as allowing for the naming of subroutines. BASIC the Seventh (1979) picked up the baton, improving SBASIC features and adding some new ones, such as the possibility of longer variables names.

The third challenge to face BASIC in the 1970s was standardization. Dartmouth was onboard with language standardization as early as 1971, when the college teamed up with Hatfield Polytechnic in England to "avoid divergent interpretations of the language by future implementors." Several years later, an American National Standards Institute (ANSI) committee called the X3J2 convened to standardize BASIC. The X3J2 broke up the language's standardization into two parts: Minimal BASIC and so-called Full BASIC. Minimal BASIC ultimately bore resemblance to the earliest versions of Dartmouth BASIC and was approved and codified in 1978. But controversy nagged the standardization of Full BASIC, centering on graphics and specialty features. It would take the committee over ten years to adopt Full BASIC standards, by which point personal computing machines, along with numerous BASIC dialects, had exploded in popularity. (The International Organization for Standardization, or ISO, also specified a set of Full BASIC standards, which was derived from the ANSI standards.) These BASIC dialects, some of which conformed to the standards, many others of which did not, caused Kemeny and Kurtz many sleepless nights; so, in part blaming themselves for not pushing for standardization much earlier, in 1983 they decided to build a ANSI-compliant, multiplatform BASIC called True BASIC. The story of True BASIC is detailed in chapter 15.

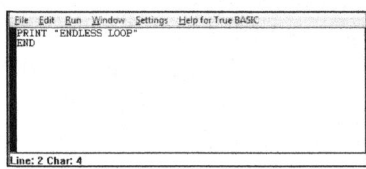

True BASIC for Windows.

Needless to say, by the middle of the 1970s control of the future of BASIC had slipped from the grasp of those at Dartmouth. There were versions of BASIC seemingly everywhere: on non-Dartmouth time-sharing terminals, on kit computers, on mainframes. Part of the problem was that programmers, in their exuberance to run BASIC on even the most underpowered machines, had cut corners; then these inferior BASICs, and the newer BASICs built off of them, had spread. Kemeny and Kurtz lauded the programming achievement of the first Microsoft BASIC—squeezing a functional BASIC into such a small amount of memory—while at the same time lambasting that implementation as detrimental to the integrity of the language itself.

Furthermore, as computers rapidly increased in power and decreased in size, hardware-dependent commands were added to implementations of BASIC, resulting in a further mishmash of the original Dartmouth vision as well as an army of incompatible BASIC implementations (i.e., a program written on one implementation might not run correctly on another). Also, the Dartmouth-GE breakup in the early 1970s left GE with a carbon copy of BASIC the Fifth on their computers, but GE didn't bother to return to Dartmouth to procure the much-improved BASIC the Sixth, to say nothing of the structured programming advances of SBASIC. BASIC the Fifth would become GE BASIC, and versions of it would spread to Digital Equipment Corporation's PDP-8 and Hewlett-Packard's HP-2000, two small computers primarily geared toward education, as well as directly into people's homes. The world was transforming.

Dartmouth was not immune to transformation, either. Kurtz, who had been the director of the Kiewit Computer Center for about a decade, recognized by 1975 that the strain on the GE computers was too great—there were too many users demanding too much computing power. He proposed that Dartmouth procure new hardware: either from GE or Honeywell, which was connected with GE. But Kemeny asked him: "What about the [advisory] Computer Council?" Had Kurtz talked with them first? The Computer Council had had enough of GE; they preferred to go with Digital Equipment Corporation, but Kurtz disagreed. Because of the dustup, Kurtz felt that Kemeny wanted him to resign as director (a meeting, sans Kurtz, was convened to discuss the matter). Kurtz complied, was instead appointed the first director of Academic Computing, and went back to doing full-time what he did best: teaching.

Kurtz may have made out fine, his legacy intact, but not everyone else was so lucky. In June of 1977, the Kiewit Computer Center had to be shut down for over ten hours after a squirrel accidently electrocuted itself in the building.

CHAPTER 6

∞

It's Not Small—It's Tiny BASIC

In 2008, Microsoft released Small Basic. But three decades before there was something much smaller: Tiny BASIC.

In was February 1976, and Bill Gates was furious. After he and Paul Allen had spent hundreds upon hundreds of hours building, refining, and copiously documenting Micro-Soft (the hyphen would later be dropped) BASIC for the Altair, he came to realize that there was a problem: although the mountains of feedback the company received about their product was by and large positive and encouraging, only about a tenth of Altair BASIC users had actually purchased the product. Gates wrote a scathing open letter to the hobbyists, those freewheeling computer tinkerers who were avidly swapping technology and tips, accusing them of copyright infringement and outright theft of his paper tape software, which cost $150: "As the majority of hobbyists are aware, most of you steal your software. Hardware must be paid for, but software is something to share. Who cares if people who worked on it get paid?" Gates continued: "[Your theft] prevent[s] good software from being written." He ended his open letter, published in the Homebrew Computer Club Newsletter (among other places)—the same Homebrew Computer Club of Silicon Valley that counted Apple Computer's two Steves (Wozniak and Jobs), as well as other future Valley luminaries, as members—with an almost sarcastic plea to "pay up." As Boisy G. Pitre and Bill Loguidice, authors of the definitive book on the Tandy TRS-80 Color Computer entitled *Co-Co: The Colorful History of Tandy's Underdog Computer* (2014), observe, "This [open] letter marked the first notable rift between the ideals of free software development and the potential of a nascent retail software market."

Bill Gates had a point. Dartmouth BASIC, although free (by the choice of its creators), was developed in an academic setting; Altair BASIC was a commercial product. The small and fledgling Micro-Soft had indeed gone all in on the Altair computer after Gates and Allen had spotted a write-up about the machine in an issue of *Popular Electronics*: the Altair landed the January 1975 cover atop the headline, "Project Breakthrough! World's First Minicomputer Kit to Rival Commercial Models," which many observers mark as the start of the personal computing revolution. The Altair looked like something out of the original *Star Trek* television series: a large box with a panel of indecipherable switches and blinking red lights. In the documentary *Triumph of the Nerds* (1996), novelist Douglas Adams memorably describes the so-called computer nerds who were attracted to the Altair: "I think a nerd is someone who uses the telephone to talk to other people about telephones. And a computer nerd, therefore, is someone who uses a computer in order to use a computer." Electronic hobbyists were buying the Altair just to use it—even if they couldn't figure out what, precisely, to use it for.

But Gates and Allen knew what to use the Altair for: they wanted to write software for the machine. But they didn't purchase an Altair; rather, they simulated one. Using a Harvard PDP-10 mainframe computer, Gates, Allen, and Monte Davidoff (a Harvard student, as was Gates at the time) had an Altair BASIC interpreter up and running in a matter of months. (Although the paper tape they used in the PDP-10 was very reliable, it was unwieldy, leading Gates and Allen to frequently drop and then have to untangle the tape.) Of course, they had made use of the PDP-10, funded by the government (and, by extension, U.S. taxpayers), free of charge to develop their fee-based BASIC; furthermore, Gates had years before logged thousands of BASIC programming hours on a GE mainframe computer hooked up to a ASR-33 Teletype terminal at the preparatory Lakeside School in Seattle instead of attending math classes. That Gates even had access to the computer was the result of, as Gates put it much later, "an incredibly lucky series of events": his birth (his father was a successful lawyer, and his mother was the daughter of a wealthy banker); attendance at a private school (Lakeside was a school for the sons and daughters of the well-heeled); and computer access (the Mothers' Club at the school had decided, the first year Gates attended Lakeside, to invest in a computer terminal; thus a computer club—in the tumultuous year of 1968, where such technology was hardly ubiquitous—was born). More important was the *type* of computer access; rather than the time delay inherent in punch cards, Gates had access to time-sharing, giving him more or less direct access to the GE computer as early as the eighth grade.

Shortly thereafter, Gates and company, including Paul Allen, worked on a PDP-10 owned by the Computer Center Corporation (C-Cubed), helping them find bugs in software in exchange for computer time. After C-Cubed went bankrupt, Gates and company landed a similar gig working on software for Information Sciences Inc. (ISI), being paid in free computer time. They programmed on weekends, nights, and during any spare moments. "It was my obsession," Gates recalled.

During Gates' senior year at Lakeside, TRW, a technology company, started building a computer network for the Bonneville Power station, but programmers were in short supply. Bud Pembroke, a founder of ISI, was contacted by TRW to see if they could help; Pembroke immediately suggested Gates and company, and the Bonneville project turned into an independent study for academic credit for Gates.

Gates wrapped up his time at Lakeside as a National Merit Scholar, having put his computer skills to clever use by coding scheduling software for the school. "It was complex, but ultimately very rewarding," Gates recalled decades later. "By the time I was done, I found that I had no classes at all on Fridays. And even better, there was a disproportionate number of interesting girls in all my classes."

After reading the article in *Popular Electronics*, Gates and Allen—who had already worked together on a commercial project called Traf-O-Data to count cars—made contact with Ed Roberts, inventor of the Altair and founder of Micro Instrumentation and Telemetry Systems (MITS), which sold the microcomputer among other electronic kits, such as model rockets (hence the word "telemetry" in the company's name) and calculators. The MITS Altair 8080 ran on an Intel 8080 microprocessor, which was similar to an earlier

Intel chip that Gates and Allen had experience with: the Intel 8008. Using assembly language, Gates, Allen, and Monte Davidoff wrote a BASIC interpreter on paper tape for the Altair (simulating the Intel 8080 on the PDP-10, similarly to how they built Traf-O-Data), and Allen flew out to MITS headquarters in Albuquerque, New Mexico, paper tape BASIC in hand along with a bootstrap loader he wrote on the plane ride, to meet in person with Ed Roberts. The night before, Allen recalled, Gates was very nervous. "Bill began to worry. What if I'd screwed up one of the numbers used to represent the 8080 instructions in the macro assembler?" Allen continued:

> Our BASIC had tested out fine on my simulator on the PDP-10, but we had no sure evidence that the simulator itself was flawless. A single character out of place might halt the program cold when it ran on the real chip. The night before my departure, after I knocked off for a few hours of sleep, Bill stayed up with the 8080 manual and triple-checked my macros.... The byte codes were correct, Bill said. As far as he could tell, my work was error-free.

Allen arrived at the airport terminal in New Mexico, looking around for Roberts. Ten minutes later, a pickup truck pulled up—it was Roberts, dressed in a short-sleeve shirt, tie, and jeans. Roberts and his company had only recently been in dire straits: MITS had been headed toward bankruptcy, with calculator sales having tanked; Roberts was in debt up to his eyeballs. MITS needed $65,000 to remain afloat. Prior to the Altair being released, Roberts had figured that no more than 800 units of the kit computer would be sold in its first year. But only a month after its release, MITS was deluged with hundreds of orders per day for the computer. Interest in the Altair was the spark that ignited the first gatherings of the Homebrew Computer Club; the Altair was a "solution in search of a problem," according to the documentary *Triumph of the Nerds*.

Ed Roberts drove Paul Allen to the MITS headquarters, which was little more than a rundown makeshift plant of a dozen workers on an assembly line located in a small building near a beauty salon. Allen loaded the BASIC interpreter into the Altair by feeding the tape into an attached Teletype machine; after a short time, Allen and Roberts were confronted with a prompt printed by the Teletype: **MEMORY SIZE?** From there, BASIC was up and running, much faster than Allen had expected it to run—since the PDP-10 with which Micro-Soft had built BASIC emulated the Altair correctly but slowly. Although not yet perfect, Allen typed in—and managed to get working—several BASIC programs, including one to print the sum of two numbers:

```
PRINT 2+2
4
```

Roberts was beside himself, screaming, "Oh my God, it printed '4'!" Next, Allen typed in the BASIC code for a lunar lander program called "ROCKET: LAND AN APOLLO CAPSULE ON THE MOON" from the David Ahl book *101 Games in BASIC* (1973). The program was short, less than two dozen lines long; the objective of the text-based game was as follows: "In this program, you set the burn rate of the retro rockets (pounds of fuel per second) every 10 seconds and attempt to achieve a soft landing on the moon." The Eagle had landed again—the program worked perfectly.

In addition to a lump-sum payment, MITS also agreed to provide Micro-Soft with royalties for every standalone copy of Altair BASIC sold (Micro-Soft produced several versions, such as the original 4K BASIC, 8K BASIC, and Extended BASIC, first on paper tape, and then later on cassette). Not pirated, but sold—which is why, recall, Gates was furious with the behavior of the hobbyists. (Later, Roberts would be furious with Gates after Micro-Soft declared their BASIC software to be proprietary and proceeded to develop it for other computers.)

But the hobbyists weren't simply going take a tongue-lashing from Mr. Gates sitting down. Gates wrote a follow-up letter addressing the many responses his first letter provoked; called "The Second and Final Letter," he wrote that "[i]n discussing software, I don't want to leave out the most important aspect, viz., the exchange of those programs less complex than interpreters or compilers that can be written by hobbyists and shared at little or no cost"—meaning that he had no problem with simple programs, built on the backs of non-free quality interpreters and compilers, being freely distributed. The hobbyists just had to stay in their lane.

But the hobbyists were more than capable of both hardware and software design, and it was only a matter of time before one of them suggested that these self-proclaimed computer-philes write their own, free-to-distribute version of BASIC. Which brings us to the birth of Tiny BASIC.

Bob Albrecht, member of the Homebrew Computer Club and founder of one of the first free computer centers for the public, was strongly opposed to the sentiments of Gates. Several years before the infamous open letter, Albrecht, along with Dennis Allison of Stanford University and George Firedrake, began the nonprofit People's Computer Company (PCC). The PCC served as the name of both a small time-sharing service and a periodic newsletter. In the Volume 3, Issue 4 PCC newsletter, titled "BUILD YOUR OWN BASIC," Dennis Allison laid out the specifications for a simplified—"fewer statements, fewer features," he said—but still functional free version of BASIC that would work on machines like the Altair (e.g., microcomputers based on the Intel 8008 or 8080). With this so-called Tiny BASIC—which was, of course, a subset of Dartmouth BASIC like Gates' version—Allison dispensed with any thought of building a compiler, which, although faster, would require more available memory storage, and focused instead of writing an interpreter. He figured a well-designed interpreter would need only a handful of kilobytes to run and could be reasonably compliant with any minimal BASIC standards.

Next, Allison enumerated the "building blocks of BASIC"—things like a line editor, line executor routine, error handling routine, and floating-point package (for working with decimals). But, in an interesting twist, Allison asks us to "[p]retend [we] are 7 years old and don't care much about floating point arithmetic (what's that?), logarithms, sines, matrix inversion (explicit matrix operations were a part of the original Dartmouth BASIC), nuclear reactor calculations and stuff like that." Instead, Allison writes, suppose you only want to use BASIC for homework, mathematics puzzles, and fun little games. With this more limited scope firmly in mind, Allison offers a proposal for a Tiny BASIC with these specs:

- No floating-point arithmetic—integers only;
- Restricted to 26 variables, with the names **A** to **Z**;

- Built-in **RND** function (a pseudorandom integer generator, necessary for most games);
- Seven BASIC statements: **INPUT, PRINT, LET, IF, GOSUB, RETURN,** and **GO TO** (two words, as in FORTRAN).
- String availability only in **PRINT** statements.

Moreover, the size of a program would be restricted to 256 lines (that's 2^8 lines), with 16 bits of integer arithmetic and no arrays.

But "BUILD YOUR OWN BASIC" wasn't a directive; rather, it was a malleable proposal, a friendly open letter circulated to a group of people who most definitely were up to the task of getting a usable BASIC interpreter off the ground so programmers had a user-friendly alternative to the drudgery of machine or assembly language coding. Allison wanted to promote the sharing of successful versions of BASIC, so he offered to spread around the interpreters, to share the wealth; "[l]et us stand on each other's shoulders, not on each other's toes," he wrote.

The call to BASIC inadvertently provided the impetus for the launch of one of the most important computer science publications: *Dr. Dobb's Journal* (the "Dobb's" is a shortened form of Dennis [Allen] and Bob [Allison]). The periodical wasn't quite called that originally, though; expected only to be a limited print run of a few issues, the superfluously titled *Dr. Dobb's Journal of Tiny BASIC Calisthenics & Orthodontia, Running Light Without Overbyte* had the express purpose of disseminating Tiny BASIC source code—starting with Dick Whipple and John Arnold's, who submitted the first Tiny BASIC interpreter, written in octal machine language, to Allison. But those first few issues proved so popular that the journal shorted its title, widened its focus beyond BASIC, and went on to be published for another four decades.

Implementations of Tiny BASIC proliferated, with perhaps the best known being Li-Chen Wang's Palo Alto Tiny BASIC, which appeared in the May 1976 issue of *Dr. Dobb's*. Wang was also a member of the Homebrew Computer Club as well as a professor; his Tiny BASIC, using less than two kilobytes of memory, even allowed for an array.

If there was a signature version of Tiny BASIC, a benchmark to measure the rest by, it was Palo Alto Tiny BASIC. Wang set or developed many of the standards that are still referenced today:

- Integers as the only permitted numbers; integers can be between 1 and 32,767 (one less than two to the fifteenth power, or 2^{15}-1);
- Twenty-six variables, from **A** to **Z** (two bytes per variable), as well as an array variable denoted by the ampersand (**&**) with indices from 1 to the remaining unused memory;
- At least three functions: in addition to **RND**, there is **ABS**, an absolute value function, and **SIZE**, which returns a count of unused bytes;
- Comparisons, such as greater than, less than, and equal to, will return either a 0 or 1 to indicate true or false, respectively;
- In addition to the seven BASIC statements listed above—**INPUT**, **PRINT**, **LET**, **GOTO** (no space between the two words), **IF** (but no associated **THEN** is required), **GOSUB**, and **RETURN**—there is also **STOP**, to halt the program, **RUN**, to read and execute program statements sequentially, **LIST**, to print out all of a program's lines, and **FOR/NEXT/STEP**, to implement loops;
- Error messages take one of three forms: (1) **WHAT?** is the interpreter's response to a garden-variety syntax error; (2) **HOW?** is the interpreter throwing up its hands in frustration, not knowing how to successfully proceed; and (3) **SORRY** is the interpreter's apology for there not being enough memory to perform a task;
- Semicolons can be used to string together statements and functions on the same program line; and
- Commas can be used in **PRINT** statements as well as in **INPUT** statements (to gather multiple inputs from the user).

Altair BASIC, which in implementation was similar to the Digital Equipment Corporation (DEC) BASIC-PLUS interpreter—unsurprising, since this was the extended dialect of BASIC Gates and Allen had grown accustomed to via the RSTS/E time-sharing system—had a number of things in common with Tiny BASIC but many differences as well. (Recall that DEC BASIC was a derivative of Dartmouth's BASIC the Fifth.) The differences between Dartmouth BASIC and the 4K and 8K implementations of Altair

BASIC are detailed in the *MITS Altair BASIC Reference Manual*'s Appendix H, which leads users through the conversion of BASIC programs not originally written for the Altair, and also in other sections of the manual. These many differences include the lengths of variable names; the assignment of array subscripts, although the **MAT** function was unavailable (Tiny BASIC did not have designated keywords for matrices); string functions for the 8K version only, such as **LEFT$, RIGHT$,** and **MID$** (string functions weren't part of Tiny BASIC); the use of a colon (**:**) to allow multiple statements per line so programs could be written in a compact, memory-saving manner; the use of the plus sign (**+**) for string concatenation; mathematical functions, such **SQR** function for taking square roots, **LOG** for finding logarithms, and **SIN, COS,** and **TAN** for trigonometry; the keywords **AND, OR,** and **NOT** for Boolean operations; and **PEEK** (returning the value of a byte to the memory) and **POKE** (writing the value of a byte to the memory) for direct access to memory. (Note that although most BASIC programmers would first encounter **PEEK** and **POKE** courtesy of Gates and Allen, the duo did not invent the two functions; rather, **PEEK** and **POKE** appeared on early DEC PDP computer operating systems like the DECsystem-10 as well as on BASIC-PLUS—the latter of which is likely where Gates and Allen learned of the two commands. **POKE** would acquire nefarious uses later on, such as employing the command to alter the contents of memory addresses to facilitate game cheats in 8-bit processors. As early as 1974, the authors of a DEC time-sharing manual recognized that the **POKE** function was a "very dangerous capability," but that wouldn't stop its spread, even to Tiny BASIC.) Most significantly, integers much bigger than Tiny BASIC allowed, in addition to floating-point numbers, were permitted (although, in the 4K version of Altair BASIC, there was in effect no difference between the two); for numerical output, the capital letter **E** was used as a stand-in for 10 to denote scientific notation.

For decades, the source code for the original 4K Altair BASIC remained under lock and key, with Bill Gates supposedly repeatedly publicly agreeing to release the source code, albeit to no avail. However, the code resides in the Harvard Library and has been disassembled; three lines of code containing remarks (comments) read as follows:

> PAUL ALLEN WROTE THE NON-RUNTIME STUFF.
> BILL GATES WROTE THE RUNTIME STUFF.
> MONTE DAVIDOFF WROTE THE MATH PACKAGE

This likely meant that Gates wrote code implementing the BASIC keywords and functions as well as memory management, while Allen wrote the tokenizer (the algorithms that translated a user's BASIC code into a compressed ID'd format to save memory) and detokenizer (the algorithms to unpack the tokenized BASIC code). In fact, BASIC source code remarks for the 6502 processor include a description of the "non-runtime stuff":

> THE CODE TO INPUT A LINE, CRUNCH IT, GIVE ERRORS,
> FIND A SPECIFIC LINE IN THE PROGRAM,
> PERFORM A "NEW", "CLEAR", AND "LIST" ARE
> ALL IN THIS AREA.

Monte Davidoff is the unsung hero of the group; a Harvard student like Gates, he was brought in to Micro-Soft for the express purpose to write the floating-point routines, which taxed even the abilities of wunderkinds like Gates and Allen. In an interview decades later, Gates recalls how the work was divvied up between the three of them:

> It was a reasonably simple instruction set. Paul was very good with the PDP-10 Assembler. I, in the meantime, laid out the design and charged off coding the BASIC. Paul later came in and helped out with that. A third person, Monte Davidoff, sat down for lunch with us and said he knew floating point packages. So, we had him write some of the math routines. And then we just kept squeezing it. So, we wrote without ever seeing [the Altair], except in this picture [the Altair image on the cover of *Popular Electronics*], and the simulator and got the BASIC running.

Also in an interview years later, Davidoff remembers that the speed at which the interpreter ran wasn't their top priority: "We weren't too concerned about efficiency. Even the 8088 then was a pretty fast processor. And we were running it over an ASR 33 Teletype running at 110 baud!" Their top priority was optimizing memory, squeezing as much as possible into as little space as possible. Regardless, Bill Gates felt like he did the lion's share of the work building the Altair BASIC interpreter. Paul Allen, who named the company Micro-Soft after dismissing such monikers as Allen & Gates—it sounded too much like a law firm—had always assumed that he and Gates were in it 50-50. Gates disagreed, demanding more than 60 percent ownership. Allen acquiesced and became a billionaire anyway.

Li-Chen Wang wasn't the only programmer to write a Tiny BASIC in opposition to Micro-Soft's. Another programmer who heeded the "BUILD YOUR OWN BASIC" call was Tom Pittman. His approach was a bit different than Wong's; instead of freely distributing the software, Pittman placed an advertisement in *Byte* magazine, asking interested parties to purchase his Tiny BASIC for the paltry sum of five dollars. "Congratulations!" Pittman wrote in the 1976 *Itty Bitty Computers Tiny BASIC User Manual*. "You have received the first of what we hope is a long line of low cost software for hobby computers. We are operating on a low margin basis, and hope to make a profit on volume."

While most other versions of Tiny BASIC were designed for the Intel 8008 or 8080 microprocessor, Pittman designed his for "other chips," as he explained in the *Dr. Dobb's* article "The Return of Tiny BASIC" (January 2006), also noting that his interpreter had an especially high fidelity to the specifications laid out originally by Allison (source code for Pittman's Tiny BASIC is printed at the end of *Dr. Dobb's* article).

Four decades on, you can still find enthusiasts, influenced by Palo Alto Tiny BASIC as well as by other variants, such as Tom Pittman's, cranking out new versions of the programming language for devices like the open-source Arduino hardware or virtual machines.

But as much as influence as the freely distributed Palo Alto Tiny BASIC had over the direction of the language, it's perhaps best remembered for promulgating an acerbic political statement. As a rejoinder to the burgeoning software market of which Bill Gates was the poster child, Wang's Tiny BASIC code listing in *Dr. Dobb's* began, in part, as follows:

BY LE-CHEN WANG.
@COPYLEFT.
ALL WRONGS RESERVED.

CHAPTER 7

∞

The Language of Superheroes

By 1980, BASIC, free of the constraints imposed on it by its creators at Dartmouth, was flying high—so high, in fact, that Supergirl herself was programming in the language.

How Supergirl became a walking advertisement for BASIC is a story of superheroes unwittingly riding the crest of a corporate wave. In the 1970s, the Tandy Corporation, a Fort Worth-based company that made its name at the turn of the century in the leather-goods business, hung its proverbial hat on one electronic device: the CB radio. Quickly ballooning to more than one-fifth of Tandy's profits by the mid-1970s, the all-the-rage CBs lured people into Radio Shack stores, thereby tempting them with a cornucopia of electronic devices both big and small. Radio Shack, which started as a small ham radio distributor in the 1920s, was acquired by Tandy in 1962. Tandy quickly exploited the Radio Shack retail chain to distribute electronics, expanding the brand by acquiring other corporations (such as Allied Radio) and merging them into a leviathan.

But some at Tandy saw the writing on the wall: the CB radio craze couldn't last forever. Sure enough, CB sales, as rapidly as they had spiked, collapsed into an abyss—and with it Tandy's profits. A replacement electronic device was needed. So, John Roach, a ten-year veteran at Tandy who had shot to vice president of manufacturing, and Don French, a buyer situated in the heart of Silicon Valley, were on a mission: bring computers to Tandy's customers.

French was an avid fan of the MITS Altair 8800, the first mass-produced microcomputer (in unassembled kit form, $395; assembled, $495) available to the public.

After visiting with companies around the country, French and Roach stumbled upon Steve Leininger, a polymath engineer who supplemented his income as a sales clerk. They lured him into the Tandy fold, but Leininger initially encountered resistance to consumer computers from corporate brass as well as a number of logistical hurdles. Eventually, though, as the CB fever broke, Leininger was given a directive: build a computer, do it cheaply, and supply Tandy with its next big thing.

In a feat worthy of MacGyver, Leininger cobbled together some parts and built a makeshift computer, loading Tiny BASIC into its tiny memory. For additional cost savings, features like lowercase characters were discarded. By early 1977, Leininger's makeshift computer, dressed to look like the future best-selling Model 1 (complete with keyboard and monitor), was ready for its close-up. Charles Tandy, Chairman of the Board, got the first look, and seemed uninterested. But the chairman simply wasn't in the habit of revealing his hand, telling Leininger after the presentation that it was not a matter of *if* but of *how many* Model 1 computers should be built. Opinions at Tandy varied widely, because with the exception of the Altair, it was hard to arrive at a predicted sales figure based on no industry data. Bernie Appel, Tandy's president, wanted to keep production volumes low (he had been opposed to the project from the start). Others wanted more produced. Eventually, it was decided: one computer for every Radio Shack store, which amounted to around 3500 units.

By August of 1977, Leininger had designed the hardware for multiple prototypes, established a software applications group with fellow employee Van Chandler, and at the last-minute strung together a version of BASIC that was originally supposed to have been coded by a consultant—who unexpectedly flew the coop.

The Warwick Hotel in New York City was the location of the unveiling of the newly-minted TRS-80 Model 1 (the "TRS" stood for Tandy Radio Shack), with its powerful Zilog Z80 CPU 8-bit microprocessor (the "80" was a reference to the chip); Tandy's presentation went off without a hitch, and the response was strong (but not immediately; people were distracted by a terrorist attack in the city which occurred earlier that same day). Tandy ended up fielding boxes and boxes of customer mail asking all sorts of questions about the TRS-80, but those questions would be answered quickly, since, through their Radio Shack stores, Tandy had a distribution center for a product that was ready for shipment immediately. And, unlike machines such as the Altair, the TRS-80 would automatically arrive fully assembled, but even a bare-bones TRS-80 would cost around $400.

Thousands upon thousands of machines were sold in those first few months; Tandy couldn't produce TRS-80s quickly enough to satisfy the demand. By 1978, Tandy had cued up their factories to manufacture more than ten thousand units per month. Tandy's marketing department followed suit, drumming up more business through "computer barnstorming" demonstrations around the country as well as masses of advertising. And more than just computer hobbyists were interested; businesses and schools also came calling, wanting more powerful computers and better software.

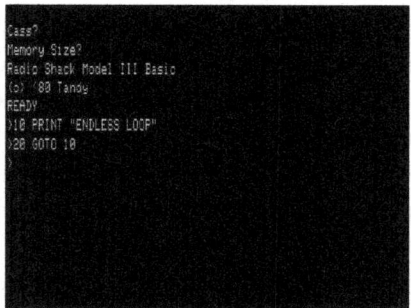

Model III BASIC for the TRS-80.

The TRS-80 initially came standard with Level I BASIC, a stripped-down version of the language, based off of Palo Alto Tiny BASIC, stored on a 4K ROM chip. Microsoft then fashioned their own BASIC interpreter, called Level II BASIC, for the TRS-80; additional memory was installed (12K of ROM), but it wasn't nearly enough, so a new version of the computer was in order: the Model II (the Model I only acquired the retronym "Model I" at the release of the Model II). But due to nagging reliability issues, that first generation of the TRS-80 had acquired an unfortunate, but memorable, nickname: Trash-80. The FCC agreed with the critics, deeming the Model I unfit because of radio frequency (RF) emissions. The nickname stuck with successive generations of the machine, despite the many improvements that came with the Model II and especially the Model III, a powerful machine that could even display lower-case characters (but it did not have the ability to display colors on-screen, which the Apple II had pioneered years before; color would ultimately arrive with the TRS-80 Color Computer, nicknamed the CoCo. Microsoft produced a new BASIC, called Color BASIC, for the CoCo's ROM). With its surfeit of software and easy means of distribution through Radio Shack stores, the TRS-80 sold very well.

Realizing that getting kids hooked as young as possible on their TRS-80s—trying to turn Trash-80 into Treasure—would result in a revenue stream for years to come, early in the life of the TRS-80 Tandy enlisted none other than the artists and writers at DC Comics to help the staff at the Radio Shack Education Comic Book Program sketch out a plan. The result was a series of embarrassing comic books starring The TRS-80 Computer Whiz Kids. Oh, and also Supergirl, Superman, and Wonder Woman.

The Computers That Saved Metropolis! (1980) finds Superman apparently moonlighting as a sixth-grade computer science teacher, explaining all sorts of esoterica while selling the benefits of the TRS-80: "Little computers like the TRS-80 can perform calculations, solve problems, play games, compare and analyze information," he explains. Superman apparently "knows" the actual sixth-grade classroom teacher, Ms. Wilson, in some unexplained way (should Lois be jealous?); two of the students in the class, Alec and Shanna, are the pseudonymous Whiz Kids. Then Superman is needed to stop a runaway tornado, and other abject silliness ensues. Luckily, two super-powerful Model 1s, as well as the Whiz Kids, are available to help avert a series of calamities.

But that's not the end of it. In *Victory By Computer* (1981), Supergirl gets into the act, too, only after Superman is grilled by the middle schoolers: "Excuse me, Superman—last time you brought along a TRS-80 under each arm—but it looks like this time you've brought *nothing* along to show us!" they whine. As if a superhero visit wasn't enough. But Superman does have something for them: a TRS-80 Pocket Computer, "six ounces of big computing power." The Pocket Computer actually wasn't a miniaturized TRS-80, but a rebranded Sharp or Casio model with a single-line LCD dot-matrix display; however, unlike its lesser calculator brethren, the Pocket Computer was truly programmable, having a limited version of

BASIC at the ready, a built-in QUERTY keyboard for convenience, and access to peripherals like printers and compact cassette recorders. The machine could run applications or perform calculations using command line inputs in Run mode. Also unlike its namesake and big brother, the Pocket Computer didn't use a Z80 microprocessor. In one panel of *Victory By Computer*, Supergirl can clearly be seen typing in a line of BASIC code in Prog (program) mode—with her other-worldly manicured fingernails hovering over the keyboard—on a pristine TRS-80 Pocket Computer; her line of code has a double-**INPUT** structure, with variables separated by commas.

Print advertisements for the Pocket Computer, such as the one on the back of the May 1983 issue of *Popular Computing*, put the machine's BASIC programmability power front and center:

> The PC-4 [a Casio rebrand] goes beyond mere programmable calculators because it features the most popular computer language—BASIC. Common commands like **GOSUB**, **LIST**, **STEP**, and up to 13 others can be entered just by pressing two keys. Numeric accuracy is 10 digits. String variables can be up to 30 characters in length, and string commands include **LEN**, **MID** and **VAL**. There's a 12-character alphanumeric display, yet program lines can be up to 62 characters long.

The popularity of the Pocket Computer paved the way for another Tandy portable computer rebranding effort in the early 1980s, this time with a Kyocera Corporation device which became TRS-80 Model 100—complete with a large LCD display, a fast processor and generous memory for its time, and fully functional, although not quite perfect, Microsoft BASIC 80 loaded into ROM. The issue of *Popular Computing* mentioned above reviewed the Model 100, pointing out its BASIC quirks: "One great surprise about BASIC is its editor; it's not the limited, line-oriented editor familiar to anyone who has programmed in Microsoft BASIC, but rather the TEXT program itself." (The TEXT program offered users rudimentary text-editing features.) The article goes on to criticize the nonintuitive manner of copying and pasting lines from one BASIC program to another, a compromise with the software made to conserve memory. "This aspect of the Model 100's BASIC will probably cause quite a few headaches among users unfamiliar with the machine.... Model 100 owners will soon learn to save programs on cassette to avoid changing them accidently." Regardless, these small computers sold well enough for Radio Shack to adopt a new tagline: "The biggest name in little computers."

Following Superman and Supergirl, Wonder Woman landed her own TRS-80 comic book: *The Computer Masters of Metropolis* (1982). Thereafter, eight more comics made the rounds, the final one released in 1992. By then, Ms. Wilson and the Whiz Kids no longer had to share the stage with the DC Comics superheroes, who had shamefacedly slunk away, compromised and flushed from embarrassment at their participation in such an obviously corporate gig.

CHAPTER 8

The Breakout Breakthrough

Bill Gates wasn't the only teenager first exposed to programming in the late 1960s.

Born in 1950 in San Jose, California, Steve "Woz" Wozniak had an abiding interest in electronics from as early as he could remember. By the time he was a high school student in Sunnyvale, his electronics teacher, Mr. McCollum, had run out of things for the young Wozniak to do—so he sent him to a company in Sunnyvale called Sylvania to learn how to program in FORTRAN on the company's IBM computer.

But it was BASIC that piqued Wozniak's interest. Unlike with FORTRAN, his first exposure to BASIC was very brief. Although there was no computer at his high school, some salesmen from GE stopped by the school to promote their time-sharing service, lugging around a modem and a Teletype terminal to demonstrate it. In the few days he had access to it, Wozniak and several other highly motivated (and math-oriented) students pounded out several short and simple BASIC programs. Wozniak didn't encounter BASIC again until after college.

The Silicon Valley Homebrew Computer Club met Wednesday evenings in an auditorium rented out by Stanford University. Computer engineer Lee Felsenstein organized and chaired the frequently raucous meetings; Wozniak was a regular attendee. (Wozniak had been at the very first Homebrew meeting, held in Gordon French's garage in Menlo Park; the meeting inspired Wozniak to build the Apple I.) Although Wozniak was very shy, usually failing to raise his hand to speak, he let the quality of his work do the talking: interested hobbyists would frequently gather around his hardware creations in awe. "In the Homebrew [C]omputer [C]lub we had a couple of books going around that I like to call 'bibles,'" Wozniak reminisced. "One was *Computer Lib/Dream Machine[s]* by Ted Nelson, describing a future world of hyperlinks to further the meaning of things in writing. His ideas were like science fiction but we all knew that they were achievable, technically, and we were all apostles for this way of looking at the future of computing. The other 'bible' was a book *101 Games in BASIC*."

101 Games in BASIC, later republished as *BASIC Computer Games*, is a collection of type-in BASIC computer games, replete with cartoon illustrations, edited by David Ahl, the founder of *Creative Computing* magazine, a popular periodical published from 1974 to 1985. (Type-ins are the source code for programs, fully printed in books or magazines, that a reader is required to literally type in to run; type-ins were most often program listings written in the BASIC language.) The programs in *BASIC Computer Games* are very generic and thus can run in most BASIC dialects with few changes. Early in his career, after completing several degrees, including a doctorate in educational psychology, Ahl was hired by Digital Equipment Corporation (DEC) to develop a series of educational products; he also edited the company's educational newsletter, *EDU*. By the early 1970s, Ahl had developed an overriding interest in computer games. He decided to port over several games written in FOCAL, an interpreted language that ran on DEC's PDP-8 computers, to BASIC—and he printed the BASIC source code in his *EDU* newsletter. These type-ins proved quite popular—especially games such as *SPACWR* (read "Space War," its abbreviated title serving as the program's file name), which later became *Super Star Trek*, a complex text-based adventure game, hundreds of lines long, involving characters from the original television series that wasn't introduced with *SPACWR* but was codified by Ahl, since there were already many versions circulating on a variety of computing platforms (the game had originated in HP's time-sharing system)—resulting in a deluge of requests for more such BASIC games. So, Ahl put out a public call for more programs to publish and received many reader submissions, some even from high school students. Ahl went on to write a number of other BASIC "cookbooks"—such books printed line-by-line recipes of code—satisfying the demand that came with the late-1970s home microcomputer popularity explosion. *BASIC Computer Games* became the first computer book to sell over a million copies.

When Wozniak first encountered Ahl's "bible," he was in his mid-twenties, working at Hewlett-Packard (HP) designing chips for calculators. But he also was dreaming of building his own home computer. Wozniak figured that a microcomputer should, at a minimum, be able to play games; from there, any other applications, such as business or word-processing or engineering, would be sure to follow. "The key to games was BASIC," Wozniak realized. Bill Gates had already written BASIC for the early Intel microprocessors; Wozniak decided to follow suit and write BASIC for his still-hypothetical machine, despite having never taken a class on how to code interpreters or compilers.

Wozniak grabbed a BASIC manual from the HP storehouses and began re-learning a language he hadn't used since high school, all in an attempt to write a BASIC interpreter for the inexpensive MOS Technology 6502 8-bit microprocessor that Wozniak would be using for his nascent Apple I (he had considered, but dismissed, chips such as the Intel 8080 and Motorola 6800 because of prohibitive costs). There were differences, though, in the DEC BASIC of Ahl's "bible" and the HP BASIC Wozniak was using as a primer, differences that weren't immediately apparent to him. At DEC, there was BASIC-PLUS, made by DEC for their PDP-11 minicomputers and run on their RSTS/E time-sharing operating system, and there was also BASIC-Plus-2. (Confusingly, these products ultimately became HP's after DEC was purchased by Compaq and Compaq merged with HP.) At HP, however, there was Time-Shared BASIC, which implemented a version of Dartmouth BASIC (including the matrix operations) on HP's 2100 minicomputers; there was Rocky Mountain BASIC, a dialect divergent from Dartmouth BASIC that consolidated HP's 9845 BASIC and its expansion modules into one package, created in Colorado; and there were yet more BASIC dialects floating around that had been made for HP's computers and calculators. Interestingly, the user interface for 9845 BASIC partitioned the screen into a printout area, a prompt line, a user input line, and an error message/system status line. The advantage of this setup, which was a precursor to the interfaces of later structured BASICs (such as QBASIC and Turbo BASIC), involved more than just additional information on-screen—the interface also permitted users to change program lines in mid-execution. Ansgar Kückes, who runs a comprehensive site devoted to the HP 9845 desktop computer, connects the idea of screen partitioning to line printers:

> Since System 45 BASIC was the successor of 9830 BASIC, ... this screen partitioning mostly goes back to the 9830 implementation of BASIC, which provided only one single line of display and input in terms of a fixed alphanumeric LED display line, and used a top-mounted line printer to do the **PRINT** output. So what the 9845 system designers essentially did, was to add a scrollable printout area which works similar like the original 9830 line printer. And in fact, all **PRINT** statements in BASIC simply print to this area, leaving the other lines untouched.

To simplify things and save time—Wozniak was racing against an imaginary clock to be the first to write BASIC for the 6502, all to "get a little fame in the hobby world, like Bill Gates" and "have something to be recognized for"—he didn't code floating-point operations (i.e., arithmetic with decimals); rather, all numerical operations would require integers, which wouldn't hurt the flow or logic of games regardless. He created a syntax table that would be stored in memory, giving each symbol on the table a code. "Each line was compared, letter by letter, through this syntax table to see if there was any valid BASIC statement," Wozniak elaborated. "The word **PRINT** might be operator number 5 and **FOR** might be operator number 13, etc. A plus sign had its code too. A symbol like a minus sign might have two different codes depending on whether it was prefix (like -5) or infix (like 9-6)."

Wozniak demonstrated the first-ever working 6502 BASIC, which he sometimes referred to as "Game BASIC," at the Homebrew Computer Club, thereby gaining his bit of fame. While he was developing the Apple II, a much-improved version of the original keyboard-connected-to-a-monitor home computer, Wozniak—who had coded Atari's *Breakout*, which was effectively a next-generation version of *Pong*, in only a few days on arcade circuit boards while minimizing the number of required chips—decided to test himself again: Could he use an interpreted language like BASIC, rather than ROM chips, to produce a playable version of *Breakout*?

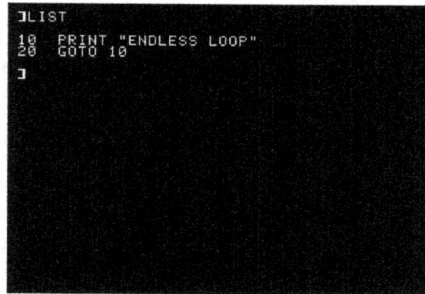
Integer BASIC for the Apple II.

If BASIC had commands to draw lines and add color, then Wozniak could do it. Therefore, he put these commands into Integer BASIC, so-called because of its lack of floating-point capability. The sixteen-color low-resolution graphics screen, made available by using the **GR** command (typing **TEXT** would return to the text-only mode), was divided into forty rows by forty columns of "bricks" (or dots or pixels), along with four lines of text available at the bottom of the screen (or forty-eight rows with no text). The **PLOT** command allowed users to draw dots. For instance, the following program plots two light blue dots: on the seventh column and third row of the screen, and then on the top left of the screen:

```
200 GR
210 COLOR=7
220 PLOT 7,3
230 PLOT 0,0
```

Replace line **210** with

```
210 COLOR=RND(16)
```

and a random color for plotting is used instead (notice that the **RND** function here produces a pseudorandom integer between 0 and 15 inclusive). If horizontal and vertical lines needed to be drawn, then the **HLIN** and **VLIN** commands, respectively, were up to the task. And the **SCRN** function returned the color of the dot at a particular row and column, which could facilitate collision detections in a videogame like *Pong* or *Breakout*. High-resolution graphics modes were available as well.

Wozniak even added a speaker with a rudimentary one-bit audio channel "just because you needed sounds when a ball hit a brick," but the unintuitive **PEEK** function had to be used in order to access the audio. Amazingly, because of the high costs associated with using a time-share assembler, he wrote Integer BASIC in machine language directly, assembling the code by hand: "The BASIC, which we shipped with the first Apple II's, was never assembled—ever. There was one handwritten copy, all handwritten, all hand-assembled. So we were in an era that we could not afford tools."

He called Steve Jobs—a younger friend from high school who he bonded with over assembling and selling illegal "blue boxes," which permitted free long-distance calls; it was Jobs who lured Wozniak over to Atari to design the original *Breakout*—over to show him the fruits of his labors; whereas making changes to an arcade game programmed on circuit boards (e.g., *Breakout*) was very time-consuming, making such changes in software (e.g., the colors of *Breakout*'s blocks) was rapid. That malleability, along with BASIC's ease of use, Wozniak and Jobs realized then, was the future of game programming.

More to the point, the Apple II was designed, in part, with *Breakout* in mind, rather than *Breakout* being shoehorned to fit within the specs of the new machine. "A lot of features of the Apple II went in because I had designed *Breakout* for Atari," Wozniak recalled, with features like color and line plotting being included because of their game-programming utility. Wozniak proudly demonstrated the Integer BASIC version of *Breakout* at the Homebrew Computer Club.

Nineteen-year-old Steve Jobs managed to procure funding for manufacturing the Apple II from the venture capitalist Arthur Rock. But when the Apple II was finally released, customers weren't happy with Integer BASIC, which was built into 5K of ROM on the computer's motherboard (and thus Integer BASIC was available with the flick of a switch, unlike BASIC for the Apple I, which had to be loaded into RAM via a cassette interface). Business applications were especially difficult to write, since working with money can't be easily done without decimal points. Microsoft had earlier offered to write floating-point BASIC for the 6502, but

Steve Jobs demurred, boasting that Apple could improve Integer BASIC over the course of a single weekend if need be; hearing the many complaints about Integer BASIC, though, Jobs first turned to Wozniak, who was busy writing a floppy disk interface for the Apple II. He finished it in time to roll out a successful demo in Las Vegas and then turned to upgrading BASIC.

But Wozniak couldn't complete the floating-point routines in time. The temperamental Jobs lost his patience and gave Microsoft the go-ahead to build floating-point BASIC for the Apple II. Wozniak still believes that his version could have been better than Microsoft's (*Call-A.P.P.L.E.* magazine, at the time, published how-to tips and tricks geared toward enhancing Integer BASIC, including hacking floating-point routines into ROM); Applesoft BASIC, Microsoft's effort (their product is sometimes also called FP BASIC), was slower and less elegant—and at first wasn't loaded into ROM; that would come later with the release of the Apple II Plus—but it had floating-point operations; even the **RND** function was altered from Integer BASIC, now only producing pseudorandom decimals between 0 and 1. Wozniak especially disliked the Applesoft's string functions **MID$** and **LEFT$**, which both return designated substrings, considering them unartful and superfluous. But Applesoft's string functions had a pedigree that dated back to Microsoft's original implementation of 4K BASIC on the Altair, which in turn bore similarity to DEC's BASIC interpreters. For instance, in the *MITS Altair BASIC Reference Manual*, the following example direct-mode 8K program (remember, inputted on a Teletype, not in front of a television screen or computer monitor) was used to demo **LEFT$**, which snags characters of a string starting with the leftmost character, and **LEN**, which relays the length of a string. First, the user had to store the string into a string variable, denoted by a dollar sign (**$**) as the last character of the variable name; notice how the **LET** keyword had become optional:

```
A$="ALTAIR 8800"
```

Then, the user was instructed to type this in:

```
FOR N=1 TO LEN(A$):PRINT LEFT$(A$,N):NEXT N
```

Which resulted in the following output:

```
A
AL
ALT
ALTA
ALTAI
ALTAIR
ALTAIR
ALTAIR 8
ALTAIR 88
ALTAIR 880
ALTAIR 8800
```

A similar example program involving **MID$**—which grabs characters from the middle of the string instead of from the leftmost or rightmost spots—was also offered:

```
FOR N=1 TO LEN(A$):PRINT MID$(A$,N):NEXT N
```

The output varied considerably from the prior direct-mode example program.

Regardless of Woz's objections, Microsoft's persistence had paid off; with Applesoft BASIC superseding Integer BASIC for many years to come, Microsoft had now established a firm foothold in the Apple world.

CHAPTER 9

∞

The Day Microsoft Almost Died

Apple was in trouble after their customers complained that Integer BASIC didn't have floating-point routines. But, by hiring Microsoft to produce Applesoft BASIC, Apple inadvertently bailed out the company from much more dire straits.

Nineteen seventy-seven was a landmark year for the nascent home computer industry. A Trinity—as *Byte* magazine famously termed it—of plug-and-play computers, computers that did not have to be assembled from a kit but were essentially ready to use at purchase, were released to the public: the TRS-80 Model I, the Apple II, and the Commodore PET, and Microsoft would provide BASIC for all three.

The Commodore PET 2001 (Personal Electronic Transactor, a backronym), so named to cash in on the pet rock craze of the 1970s, was unveiled at the Winter Consumer Electronics Show (CES) in early 1977. The machine used the same MOS Technology 6502 microprocessor that ran the Apple I. The 6502 chip had its roots earlier in the decade, in the laboratories of Motorola. There, a team of engineers crafted the 6800 microprocessor, an expensive precursor to the 6502. When Chuck Peddle, who was part of that team of engineers, left Motorola to join MOS Technology in the mid-1970s, he brought the design of the 6800 with him. Minimally tinkering with 6800's specs, Peddle helped MOS produce the 6801, a cheap version of the original microprocessor; shortly thereafter, a modified chip, the 6502, was released. And Commodore was interested.

Commodore Business Machines was founded in 1958 in Toronto by Holocaust survivor Jack Tramiel. Born Idek Tramielski, he changed his name after the Second World War. After Tramiel immigrated to the U.S. and served in the Korean War, he found work as a typewriter repairman and eventually formed a small company. Commodore originally produced typewriters, then adding machines, and then calculators, including programmable ones. But when Texas Instruments, who supplied calculator parts, decided to enter the fray as a calculator supplier themselves in 1975, Tramiel decided to purchase chip suppliers directly with the help of a key investor, Irving Gould (who was also the chairman). As part of that purchasing spree, in September 1976 MOS Technology became part of Commodore: Tramiel had effectively set in motion an existential crisis at MOS by ordering chips from the company but not paying them; this non-payment reduced MOS's capital considerably since Commodore was their biggest customer, making MOS ripe—and cheap—for a takeover. However, the acquisition also required that Peddle become head of engineering at Commodore.

Once there, Peddle (along with Andre Sousan, vice-president of engineering; Sousan coined the "PET" name) convinced Tramiel to shift Commodore's business from calculators to home computers. At MOS, Peddle had helped to design the KIM-1 single-board kit computer, which used the 6502. The PET took as its basic design the KIM-1, but placed the hardware at the center of the first-ever all-in-one home computer package, which included a monochrome monitor, a chiclet-style QWERTY keyboard with additional numeric keypad, a cassette interface, and 4K of built-in memory. The machine also doubled the standard 128 ASCII character set; the additional 128 characters were graphics symbols (e.g., playing card suits and simple geometric designs). The Commodore's entire extended character set was nicknamed PETSCII.

Commodore needed BASIC for the PET, so the company looked to Microsoft. The instruction set for the 6800 chip was similar to the 6502, so several Microsoft employees, including Bill Gates and Richard Weiland, wrote a BASIC interpreter for the microprocessor in 1976. Hearing that the Apple II used the 6502, Microsoft asked Apple if they wanted BASIC, at which point Steve Jobs callously dismissed them. So, Microsoft next turned to Commodore, which was also building a computer with the 6502 microprocessor. Gates and company landed a contract to put BASIC into the PET's ROM, rather than having to load the interpreter into RAM via external means (e.g., a cassette interface). Desperate as they were to disseminate BASIC, however, Microsoft made a mistake: failing to negotiate a per-unit fee like they had done with the Altair—Gates suggested $3 per unit; in response, Tramiel sniffed, "I'm already married"—Microsoft acquiesced to sell the product to Commodore for a flat, one-time fee of $25,000, which was to be paid only when the computer shipped. Furthermore, the Commodore license for BASIC was infinitely extendible, without additional payment or permission necessary, to any other Commodore computer with the same microprocessor. Commodore later took great advantage of this setup, repeatedly releasing versions of Commodore BASIC for their entire 8-bit home computer series—including the sequel to the PET, the VIC-20, of which William Shatner was the spokesperson in commercials, and the Commodore 64, among many others—over the course of nearly a decade. Commodore made a number of changes to Microsoft's BASIC, such as changing the **OK** prompt to read **READY** (the first version of Altair BASIC had **READY**, as did Dartmouth BASIC; later on, when Gates was "squeezing bytes out" and optimizing code, he thought it "faster to print **OK**, which is a nice, friendly word," as he explained in a 1994 video about the Altair).

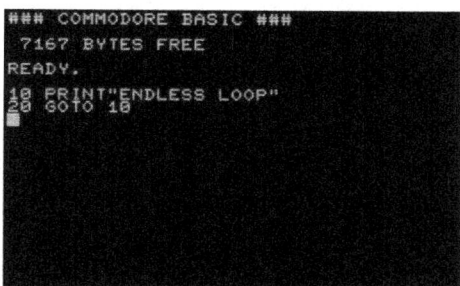

Commodore BASIC for the Commodore PET.

Years later, Gates wistfully recalled the collaboration between Microsoft and Commodore on BASIC:

> In terms of Commodore PET, they started with us from the very beginning. Because we helped Chuck Peddle, who was at Com-

modore at that time, really think about the design of the machine. Adding lots of fun characters to the character set, things like smiley faces, and suit symbols. That was the first machine we did that had this wild extended character set [i.e., PETSCII].

At the time, though, Gates knew he was getting the short end of the stick from Tramiel; to ensure that Commodore could never claim that they had written Commodore BASIC instead of Microsoft, Gates himself supposedly inserted an Easter egg into the second version of Commodore BASIC: type `WAIT6502,1` into the Commodore PET and the word `MICROSOFT!` pops up at the top left of the screen. The contract that Microsoft had with Commodore, however, did not call for the Microsoft name to be displayed anywhere on-screen, and, when Tramiel's son (who was an engineer at Commodore) saw it, he was furious with Gates for using some of the PET's precious memory for nonsense. The Easter egg was eventually removed to free up space. (Note that the Microsoft Easter egg didn't only appear in the Commodore version of BASIC, but in other implementations, including the TRS-80 Color Computer's.)

This Faustian bargain—sell BASIC but reap no long-term reward from it—put Microsoft in a precarious financial position. But Jobs, dissatisfied with Wozniak's slow progress on adding floating-point routines to the Apple II's Integer BASIC, contacted Gates—a leader Jobs respected for recognizing the importance of software and then building a successful company, Microsoft, around it. They struck a deal: the cash-strapped Microsoft would supply a BASIC implementation called Applesoft BASIC to Apple for a flat-fee immediate payment of $31,000, along with yearly payments through the length of the license—which was valid for eight years—thereby bailing Microsoft out of its self-generated mess.

But Apple wasn't in the clear yet. The BASIC that Microsoft licensed to Apple had a number of bugs. Not only did different graphics modes need to be implemented in the code, but the Apple II had no built-in assembler, forcing the programmers to work with a cross-assembler "online" (at a remote location) through a Teletype. The connection was terribly slow, so work progressed at a snail's pace; even worse, in December 1977 the company facilitating the interface, Call Computer, accidently erased all of the work Apple's programmers had completed on Applesoft BASIC, forcing

Apple to restart the project with nothing more than handwritten notes.

But Apple programmer Cliff Huston had an inspired idea: instead of using the Teletype cross-assembler to recode the interpreter, he would utilize a cross-assembler on an in-house antiquated paper-tape reading IMSAI computer, an extremely similar machine to the Altair 8800. Work proceeded apace, with Applesoft BASIC being released to the public in early 1978, on cassette and on schedule. Though it looked like Integer BASIC, Applesoft BASIC had some significant limitations: it was slow, taking long to load; it was temperamental, whereby a wrong keystroke could delete an entire program; and high-resolution graphics weren't available for use. There were, however, low-resolution graphics commands, such as for plotting squares and lines.

After patching up the code and fixing some bugs, Microsoft delivered a second version of 6502 BASIC to Apple. Programmers at Apple again got to work improving the software, adding high-resolution graphics commands and renaming the low-res commands; in addition, Applesoft II was ported to ROM for the Apple II Plus, making the loading of BASIC instantaneous.

By 1985, the shoe was on the other foot, and now Apple needed Microsoft. While the Lisa, which was named after Jobs' daughter and was the first home computer with a graphical user interface but was very expensive, and the Macintosh, which arrived a year later, were the company's focus, the Apple II was still the company's most popular product, supplying Apple with a steady stream of revenue, and thus had to continue to be supported. Part of that support involved BASIC and thus Applesoft, but Microsoft's eight-year license of the product was up, and Apple couldn't afford to gut Applesoft from the Apple II ROM—that would leave thousands upon thousands of software products inoperable. Bill Gates had Apple over a barrel. But instead of charging the company an arm and a leg to continue using Applesoft, Gates had a different idea: a trade. Apple was, in-house, developing a new version of BASIC, called MacBASIC, for the Macintosh, which had shipped without BASIC. In 1985, a beta version MacBASIC had been released and was generating buzz; MacBASIC seemed to be faster than Microsoft's BASIC, and it was even sent out to Dartmouth University to use in an introductory programming class. Gates wanted MacBASIC.

Andy Hertzfeld, employed at Apple at the time, later recalled the genesis of MacBASIC: as a port of Applesoft BASIC to the business market-oriented Apple III. (Microsoft ended up releasing its own version of BASIC for the short-lived Apple III, and so did Apple: Apple Business BASIC. Both of these implementations were of a piece with the so-called Business Basics of the 1970s and '80s, which were BASICs optimized for business use.) But by 1981, with the Macintosh project in full swing, Hertzfeld and others on the team "thought that a Basic interpreter would be important, to allow users to write their own programs. We decided we should write it ourselves, instead of relying on a third party, because it was important for the Basic programs to be able to take advantage of the Macintosh UI [user interface], and we didn't trust a third party to 'get it' enough to do it right." Within a few months, fellow team member Donn Denman had crafted a fairly complete BASIC interpreter (complete with text editor, parser, and interpreter to execute the byte code) for the proto-Mac, but the hardware kept changing, necessitating changes to the code. Although it wasn't ready in time for the January 1984 launch of the Mac, Denman redoubled his efforts to rewrite the interpreter as quickly as possible. Microsoft released a version of BASIC for the Mac, but it didn't take advantage of the Mac's unique GUI features, leaving the door wide open for Denman's interpreter, which he finished in 1985. But just as MacBASIC was to be released, Bill Gates made the deal to obtain MacBASIC in exchange for the eight-year license extension for Applesoft. Gates couldn't fathom any version of BASIC being on an Apple except Microsoft's—despite his company releasing versions of other programming languages like FORTRAN, COBOL, and Pascal by this point, BASIC was still arguably the company's bread and butter—and with Microsoft's legal ownership of MacBASIC and the outstanding beta copies recalled, MacBASIC was effectively dead and buried. Except, that is, for pirated versions of the beta, which made the rounds enough to lead to several books being published about the now-defunct interpreter.

CHAPTER 10

∞

BASIC, Widely Distributed

Microsoft made its name porting implementations of BASIC to a variety of microprocessors, from the 8080 to the Z80 to the 6502 to, eventually, the 8086. But not everyone was satisfied with Microsoft's efforts.

When the Tandy TRS-80 was ready to ship, Microsoft was not ready with their version of BASIC for the machine. So, the TRS-80 shipped with 4K Level I BASIC, a reworked version of Palo Alto Tiny BASIC that also had a cassette interface, keyboard and video support, and floating-point routines, as well as several string variables and an array variable. Error messages took the traditional Tiny BASIC form: **HOW?**, **WHAT?**, and **SORRY**. Microsoft finished Level II BASIC for the Model I and Model III in a short timeframe; Gates described Level II BASIC as a "hybrid" between the Altair's Extended BASIC and 8K BASIC, with new control structures, such as **IF/THEN/ELSE**, available, in addition to more flexibility with working with numbers such as integers and double-precision variables. Most significantly, Level II BASIC gave users easy access to graphics commands such as **SET** (used to draw a small graphics block at designated *x-y* coordinates), **RESET** (used to erase a small graphics block), and **POINT** (used to test if a particular block at some set of coordinates is lit, especially useful for videogame collision detections). What's more, a new function to test for real-time keyboard input, called **INKEY$**, was added; the old **INPUT** statement, which paused the interpreter to wait for user input, was no longer sufficient. As David A. Kater and Susan J. Thomas, in their book *TRS-80 Graphics for the Model I and the Model III* (1982), explain it,

> The **INPUT** statement is not adequate for real-time keyboard control of motion. Every time an **INPUT** is executed, the screen display freezes in anticipation of operator input.... The **INKEY$** function continually strobes the keyboard. When a key is depressed, the ASCII value of that key is stored in the **INKEY$** buffer. Because this buffer is only one byte long, each time a new key is depressed, its ASCII value replaces the one previously stored in the buffer. So we can test the buffer for the ASCII value of the last key to be depressed.

Tandy also released an enhanced version of the interpreter for the TRS-80 called Disk BASIC.

In reflecting on the Model II, which was designed as a business, rather than a home, microcomputer, Gates waxed nostalgic in a 1981 interview with *80-U.S. Journal*, the TRS-80-exclusive magazine that later changed its name to *Basic Computing*. "Well, the idea there was that the Model II people were probably more businessman. The spare time to be curious and really learn about it didn't come into it as much." Thus, **PEEK** and **POKE** weren't included in the Model II's BASIC.

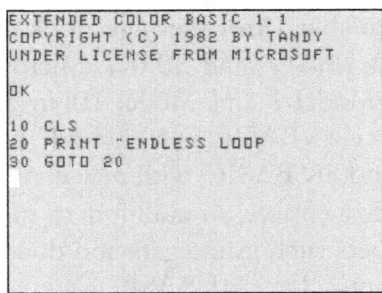

Color BASIC for the TRS-80 Color Computer.

When Tandy shipped the much-anticipated TRS-80 Color Computer—the screen displayed a cursor that continually flashed colors—the **SET** statement would get an upgrade for Microsoft Color BASIC: there would be parameters not only for the x and y coordinates, but also for the color of the particular graphics block. In addition, high-resolution graphics, albeit with a palette of fewer available colors, was possible, and a simple function, called **JOYSTK**, read the position of the available joysticks. Color BASIC was squeezed into 8K of ROM; go the Extended Color BASIC route, as many did, and 16K of memory was required (16K, along with Extended Color BASIC, was shipped standard with the CoCo 2). In the same *80-U.S. Journal* quoted above, Gates touted the features Color BASIC, mentioning 3D graphics and a color-mixing **PAINT** algorithm. But he ended the interview on an ominous note. "The only real threat to it [the Color Computer] is if Commodore can get their act together. It is possible that they could be a serious competitor," he says. "I'm interested to see if Commodore follows through."

Commodore BASIC went through a number of iterations, but—even unmoored from Microsoft—they all hewed fairly closely to Microsoft's original. When Commodore BASIC version 2 booted up from ROM, the top of the screen displayed the system RAM (typically 64K) and the number of bytes free to work with in BASIC (typically 38,911), along with the interpreter's patient **READY** prompt. The **LOAD** command would load a BASIC program from permanent storage (e.g., a cassette or a disk) to RAM, while the **SAVE** command would save a program from RAM to permanent storage. The reserved BASIC keywords were of a piece with Altair BASIC's, with special tokens like the question mark (**?**) abbreviating the **PRINT** statement—which was fairly standard on BASICs by then—and shifted characters standing in for other commands and statements (e.g., **GOTO** abbreviated by shift-G)—which was not common, although Level I BASIC on the TRS-80 also permitted abbreviated keywords to save memory since statements were not tokenized (i.e., keywords were stored in their entirety). In order to save memory, Commodore BASIC programmers tended not to put spaces in their lines of code—since blank spaces were not removed by the tokenizer and thus cost programs extra precious bytes.

The Commodore BASIC text editor was very flexible, with arrow keys permitting the user to edit program lines rapidly rather than resorting to **EDIT** commands; the chicklet keyboard even had a user-friendly RUN/STOP key. Like Applesoft BASIC, though, graphics commands were the bane of Microsoft's BASIC efforts; version 2.0 of Commodore BASIC, Microsoft's last iteration for the Commodore PET, had no graphics or sound keywords. To conjure up visuals, BASIC programmers had to be creative, eventually realizing that **CHS$**, a function to display ASCII characters, could be put to artistic purposes. (More intrepid programmers resorted to machine language routines.) The famous one-line program that generates an aesthetically pleasing infinite maze built of PETSCII characters,

```
10 PRINT CHR$(205.5+RND(1));:GOTO 10
```

inspired a 2012 MIT Press multi-author book of essays offering meditations on graphical output, music, dance, randomness, and computers in general—with the mouthful of a title *10 PRINT CHR$(205.5+RND(1)); : GOTO 10*, which will hereafter be referred to as simply *10 PRINT*—is a testament to the Commodore community's creativity in the face of limitations.

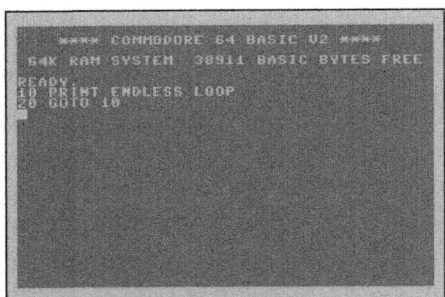

Commodore BASIC for the Commodore 64.

Eventually, multimedia features would be added to Commodore BASIC, and they would be worth the wait, with sprite manipulation (courtesy of **PEEK** and **POKE**, although you had to be especially careful when you **POKE**d a PET: a so-called Killer **POKE** was possible, which was a one-line command that could potentially damage hardware—in this case, the CRT monitor; and a Killer **POKE** on the later Commodore 64 might cause damage to the external floppy drive. These Killer **POKE**s are similar to the record player in Hofstadter's *Gödel, Escher, Bach*: when the phonograph plays a certain recording, the record's frequency vibrations cause the machine to break), joystick access, and sound features part of later versions, making Commodore BASIC one of the most game-friendly computers to program. Commodore even managed to optimize the functionality of the **GOTO** statement, having it know when to search from the current location of the program's execution instead of from the very first line in the program downward, depending on which process was faster.

By the early 1980s, users interested in adding an array of BASIC features, especially screen commands, could opt for Simons' BASIC, distributed as a ROM cartridge. As the story goes, Simons' BASIC was written by a precocious British sixteen-year-old who had received a Commodore as a gift on his thirteenth birthday and then proceeded to "[survey] other Basics and their extensions and picked from among their features," according to a *Creative Computing* article written at the time. The Commodore 64 ended up becoming the best-selling 8-bit computer of all time.

At Apple, dissatisfaction with Applesoft led to efforts to improve the software or replace it altogether. Utility programs called the Beagle Compiler, which created an executable binary file of an Applesoft program, and MD-BASIC, which optimized Applesoft programs, allowing them to work on any Apple II as well as adding conditional statements and looping structures, both improved the end-user experience. There was AC/BASIC, a compiled version of the BASIC language, sans line numbers, that was made available for the Commodore Amiga as well. And Micol Advanced BASIC also compiled programs without requiring line numbers.

Then there was Texas Instruments (TI). TI didn't start as a computer company. Right around the time of the Second World War, Texas Instruments, then called Geophysical Service, had its proverbial finger in many pies. TI was involved with seismic exploration and electronics, looking to expand to semiconductors and transistors. By the mid-1950s, TI had produced the first transistor radio on the heels of Bell Labs' physicists Walter Brattain and John Bardeen, under the loose direction of William Shockley, who had made the semiconductor breakthrough at Bell Labs.

Although the transistor, made of semiconductor materials such as germanium, was a monumental leap over the vacuum tube, there was still much room for improvement, Jack Kilby of TI realized. So Kilby assembled the first microchip, a collection of numerous transistors all stitched haphazardly together. (Robert Noyce, later a co-founder of Intel, produced a cleaner, printed circuit version at Fairchild Semiconductor six months after Kilby.) Kilby was then recruited by the higher-ups at TI to design a lightweight and cheap handheld calculator that could do what the weighty and expensive calculators chained to office desks could do. From these efforts, the SR-10 and SR-50, handheld calculators with red LED displays that were nonetheless (with a hint of skeuomorphism) named after slide rules (SR), were born. Expanding their electronics division even further, TI produced watches and digital clocks and toys—and computers.

In 1979, to compete with the Trinity, TI released the TI-99/4, the first 16-bit home computer available in the U.S. market. The microprocessor was a Texas Instruments TMS9900 originally built for the TI-990 series of minicomputers. Microsoft was contracted to build BASIC for the TI-99/4, and the two lead programmers, Bob Wallace and Bob Greenberg, struggled to get it done, in part because TI only supplied Microsoft with a TI interpreter to write the language in—making TI BASIC a member of the rare breed of double-interpreted languages. In recounting what a task-master Bill Gates could be, Paul Allen noted that Bob Greenberg, who had also attended Harvard, worked over eighty hours in the span of four days, Monday to Thursday, to finish TI BASIC, but Gates' reaction was to simply ask him, "What are you working on tomorrow?"

TI BASIC was a limited but easy to use implementation of the language, devoid of many of the features of the 1977 Trinity's versions. Later, a TI Extended BASIC ROM cartridge—created by TI—brought TI BASIC up to par. Subprograms, sprites, and speech synthesis using the **CALL SAY** command (the TI Speech Synthesizer hardware, utilized in such toys as the Speak & Spell, was required), set TI Extended BASIC apart from the pack.

By the early 1990s TI's computer business was foundering but their graphing calculator division was booming. Calculators such as the TI-81 and -82, and later TI graphing calculators, made use of an interpreted implementation of BASIC; this version was limited in its scope but could (and still can) handle a number of standard control statements, such as **If** statements and **For** loops, along with different data types including lists and matrices (which can be manipulated in the calculator outside of the programming environment). TI-BASIC, one of only two options for programming on the TI graphing calculators (the other is assembly), is free of line numbers; instead, each statement begins with a colon (:). Since TI's graphing calculators are commonly used in schools and are required on many standardized tests, many students' first (and perhaps only) exposure to the BASIC programming language comes courtesy of TI-BASIC.

Atari also once manufactured personal computers. Nolan Bushnell and Al Acorn founded Atari in 1972, really for only one reason: to develop and release the arcade version of *Pong*, a game with a simple directive—"Avoid missing ball for high score"—that was virtually a carbon copy of one of the Magnavox Odyssey's "Tennis" games, which Bushnell had seen at a Magnavox demo months earlier. Despite being sued for copyright infringement, Atari would blossom through the decade, releasing arcade hits such as *Breakout* (which Atari employee Steve Jobs was assigned to optimize, only to secretly turn the task over to his friend and HP employee Steve Wozniak) and *Asteroids*. By 1979, spurred on by the Trinity's success, Atari, like Texas Instruments, released a home computer in two trims: the Atari 400 and the Atari 800. The design of the computer began two years before with the release of the Atari 2600 home videogame console. Similar to the 2600, the 400 and 800 would be 8-bit machines running off of a MOS 6502 microprocessor. (Interestingly, also in 1979 Atari released a non-gaming ROM cartridge for the 2600 called *BASIC Programming*, a very limited BASIC interpreter and dynamic tutorial. When run, the screen was split into six horizontal regions: Program, permitting less than a dozen BASIC lines (input via special Keyboard Controllers); Stack, displaying intermediate results; Variables, showing the values of variables; Output, displaying the output; Graphics, showing two polygons; and Status, a real-time display of the available memory. Some sophisticated mathematics was possible, such as modular arithmetic. The Atari *BASIC Programming* manual contained source code for several sample programs, including two versions of *Pong*. Inspired by *BASIC Programming*, several years later Nintendo released its own cartridge BASIC dialect called *Family BASIC* for the Japanese Family Computer.)

At first, Atari purchased Microsoft 8K BASIC for the 6502, intending to expand the code and optimize it to work with the proprietary hardware while still being able to fit it snugly into an 8K ROM cartridge (BASIC would not be built into ROM for the Atari 400 and 800, unlike later Atari computers such as the 600XL and 800XL). Struggling with the (undocumented by Microsoft) code and short on time before the upcoming unveiling of their new home computer at the CES, Atari turned to Shepardson Microsystems, who had built Apple's DOS (and was also initially contracted to write BASIC for the Apple II as part of a product called Apple Lanny, which was cancelled), to finish the job. Shepardson decided to throw out Microsoft's code completely and start building a BASIC interpreter for Atari from scratch, and Atari BASIC was completed on time for the CES. Atari BASIC uses a tokenizer, handles strings differently than Microsoft BASIC (e.g., there are no string arrays, since the characters that make up the string *is* the array), offers support for graphics, sound, and peripherals like joysticks, and, uniquely at the time, makes use of a line editor that dynamically checks for syntax errors, line by line, after each press of the ENTER key (before running the program). Many of the differences between Microsoft BASIC and Atari BASIC can be chalked up to their inspiration: while Microsoft built its original Altair BASIC off of Digital Equipment Corporation's BASIC-PLUS interpreter, Shepardson used Data General's (DG) Business Basic as the source. While Bill Gates was familiar with DEC's interpreter thanks to thousands of hours of time-sharing practice logged as a teenager, Shepardson's developers, Kathleen O'Brien and her husband, Paul Laughton, were more comfortable with DG because of a time-sharing system Laughton had worked on at IBM.

But Business Basic, which ran on DG's Nova minicomputers, wasn't capable of floating-point operations. So, O'Brien was made responsible for Atari BASIC's floating-point routines, while her husband handled the rest of the implementation. "I didn't know how to do floating point and Bill Wilkinson explained what was needed for floating point and then I implemented it," she recalled decades later. As for Bill Wilkinson, he was given credit in Atari BASIC source code comments, but he ultimately wasn't fond of how strings were handled: "I don't like the way the length of the string is defined in Atari BASIC," he said. Continuing,

> In Cromemco BASIC the length of the string is defined by the number of characters, up to and including the last null characters.

So if you attach nulls onto the end of a string it will automatically shorten. Obviously that is a better definition than the Atari version. Inputs should have been able to handle quotes, an oversight.

O'Brien enjoyed the work, but the team's schedule was grueling, having to put in multiple fourteen-hour days in a row, clocking out past midnight, simply to meet the hellacious deadlines (typical of the computer industry at the time). But because Laughton had earlier worked on the defunct Apple Lanny project for the Apple II, he had the basics of BASIC covered, and was ready for the peculiarities of Atari's implementation.

In 1981, Optimized Systems Software (OSS), cofounded by Bill Wilkinson, purchased several products from Shepardson, including Atari BASIC. OSS immediately got to work improving the BASIC implementation, releasing BASIC A+, an extension of Atari BASIC, shortly thereafter. Text formatting was improved, along with better error code communication on-screen, but the included print documentation was widely considered inadequate. BASIC A+ was followed by two more OSS implementations: BASIC XL and BASIC XE, both offering further improvements through the remainder of the life of the Atari home computer line.

German programmer Frank Ostrowski released an interpreter-compiler called Turbo-Basic XL, which addressed a number of issues with other Atari BASIC implementations—most notably, speed. Atari BASIC was notoriously slow. Around that time, author David Ahl wrote a short "Simple Benchmark" program for *Creative Computing* that was used to test various implementations of BASIC; when run, the eleven-line program would print out only two floating-point numbers, but those two numbers were the result of a set of calculations involving nested loops (i.e., loops within loops), square roots, absolute values, powers, and random number generation. While implementations of Microsoft BASIC would typically use a tokenized stack architecture to handle such situations, Atari BASIC dealt with loops in a suboptimal manner and wasn't much quicker at resolving math routines, thus taking quite a while to run Ahl's "Simple Benchmark" program to completion. Regardless, eventually Atari managed to fit a version of Microsoft BASIC into an 8K cartridge, after first releasing it in (much slower) disk form, bringing the story of BASIC on the Atari full circle.

CHAPTER 11
∞
Microsoft, IBM, and the Clones

Doubts ran high that IBM could compete in the personal computer market. In fact, one analyst memorably said, "IBM bringing out a personal computer would be like teaching an elephant to tap dance." But when the elephant began tap dancing, Big Blue's critics had to eat crow.

IBM began as a loose confederation of a variety of business, such as electronic-tabulating and time-clock machines, at the turn of the twentieth century. Quickly ascending to head the consolidated, newly christened IBM, Thomas Watson led the company for its first four decades; he oversaw the company's first forays into the nascent computer industry. Then his son, Thomas Watson, Jr., took over. Both Watsons demanded fierce loyalty from their employees; the company even published a song book with paeans to IBM and its leadership.

IBM could scarcely imagine a computer market then beyond one hundred or so businesses, all employing machines whose physical bulk was as intimidating as its means of operation was opaque. A small user-friendly computer for every man, woman, and child? Completely out of the question.

By the mid-1960s, Big Blue had become a leader in supplying huge mainframe computers for commercial, scientific, and governmental applications—including partnerships with NASA—

notably with their IBM System/360 and IBM System/370. But by the 1970s, IBM was losing market share to companies such as DEC, causing Big Blue to rethink their strategy with respect to computers in general.

Two years before the Trinity, IBM released the IBM 5100 "portable" computer. Although it wasn't a kit computer à la the Altair, the reason why the 5100 is mostly forgotten is because of its size and price: though it was technically portable, it weighed almost 60 pounds and cost anywhere between $10,000 and $20,000. Plus, it was not marketed for the home user, but for industrial end-users with limited or no access to IBM's large mainframe computers. The 5100 was a mainframe for the road. The IBM 5100's successors, though, the 5110 and the 5120, were targeted to a different end-user: office workers. But the 5100's problems of bulk and price remained.

The company's first successful microcomputer, the IBM Personal Computer (PC), also called the IBM 5150, which was released in 1981, has a storied history. Getting wind of IBM's burgeoning interest in the home computer market, Atari made IBM's CEO Frank Cary an offer in 1980: Atari would build a PC for IBM, effectively putting an IBM logo on an Atari 800 clone. Bill Lowe, the director of IBM's development lab, which was based in Boca Raton, Florida, spoke for Cary when he dismissed the idea outright. Instead, Lowe volunteered to assemble a team that would release a viable PC in about a year—and, furthermore, he wouldn't need to retain hundreds of employees to do it.

Lowe brought together a nimble team of only twelve people for the project. Don Estridge was put in charge; Estridge designated Jack Sams to take care of the software for the PC. Sams realized that with a one-year launch deadline, there simply wasn't enough time to fashion the requisite parts and programs internally, so he looked outside the company. Sams had his pulse on the home computer market, and he was especially impressed by one vendor: Microsoft. "We didn't think we could introduce a product that could out-BASIC Microsoft's BASIC," he recalled. So Sams called up Microsoft, hoping to schedule a meeting with Bill Gates. Gates initially tried to put him off, but to no avail: Sams told him that he was already on his way to the airport to fly to Seattle.

When Sams arrived (along with two IBM executives), he was greeted by the curious sight of a baby-faced Gates, wearing an oversized suit. "This young fellow came out to take us back," Sams later remembered, "and I thought he was the office boy." Gates won Sams—and Big Blue—over in a freewheeling conversation about all aspects of the PC industry at Microsoft's headquarters. Sams' interest in licensing Microsoft BASIC ballooned into licensing every programming language Microsoft had on offer—even if Microsoft hadn't technically programmed all the implementations yet. In other words, Gates bluffed, pretending he had a large product line of programming languages when he only had a small one. Sams also consulted with others besides Gates in the home computer industry.

Roughly a month after forming the team, Bill Lowe presented a proposal to IBM brass for the IBM PC. Instead of going with the 6502 or Z80 8-bit microprocessors of other microcomputers on the market, the IBM 5150 would jump a generation to an Intel 8088; the 8088 was a hybrid between an 8-bit and a 16-bit processor. To keep costs down and customers satisfied, the PC would also have an "open architecture," meaning that the machine would have a plethora of options and required parts could be outsourced to vendors to supply. The customer could design the product she needed, but with that extreme flexibility came IBM's need to relinquish end-to-end control—something that, notoriously, Apple's Steve Jobs was becoming less and less willing to do with his products (e.g., the forthcoming Macintosh, unlike the Apple II with its many expansion slots). Perhaps Big Blue's philosophy of cobbling together the best of what was out there, the tried-and-true, rather than reinventing the wheel, was best summarized by Don Estridge in an interview with *Byte* several years after the release of the PC. "IBM has an excellent BASIC—it's well received, runs fast on mainframe computers, and it's a lot more functional than microcomputer BASICs were in the 1980s," he began.

> But [its] number of users were infinitesimal compared to the number of Microsoft BASIC users. Microsoft BASIC had hundreds of thousands of users around the world. How are you going to argue with that? Many who wrote about the IBM PC at the beginning said that there was technologically nothing new in this machine. That was the best news we could have had; we actually had done what we had set out to do.

IBM brass was duly impressed with the PC proposal—codenamed Project Chess—and the team was given one year to make their PC, codenamed Acorn, a reality. Another problem now cropped up: What operating system should be used? Sams went back to Microsoft, presenting his current thinking to Gates. Perhaps there should be two choices, he said: Boot up to BASIC from ROM, or let the disk operating system (DOS) called Control Program/Monitor (CP/M) handle the chores. Microsoft already had an implementation of BASIC (complete with **PEEK** and **POKE** and graphics commands), called MBASIC, for the CP/M operating system up and running on portable computers such as the Osborne 1; MBASIC was a derivative of Microsoft BASIC-80, a BASIC tailored for the Z80 microprocessor and itself a direct descendant of Altair BASIC. CP/M was a product of Digital Research (its founded name was Intergalactic Digital Research), a company operated and owned by the mild-mannered Gary Kildall, a childhood friend of Gates. Digital and Microsoft had maintained an informal partnership for years: if a company was in the market for an operating system, Microsoft would kindly suggest CP/M (which had already sold hundreds of thousands of copies), and if another company required a programming language implementation, Digital would refer them to Microsoft.

Around 1979, however, trust between the two companies broke down after Digital released a version of CP/M containing a BASIC implementation not written by Microsoft. This non-Microsoft BASIC was called CBASIC, written by Gordon Eubanks, a naval officer who had attended the Naval Postgraduate School in California with Kildall. Eubanks initially wrote BASIC-E as his master's thesis; BASIC-E was based on a CP/M BASIC compiler programmed by Kildall, who had a doctorate in computer science. CBASIC, which was an evolution of BASIC-E, improved on MBASIC's handling of decimal numbers and was expressly designed with commercial applications in mind.

Nevertheless, Gates still referred IBM's Sams to Digital, but things began to breakdown quickly from there. When Sams and his IBM team arrived at Digital, he wasn't greeted by Kildall, but by his wife, who also happened to be Digital's business manager, Dorothy McEwan; Kildall was out flying his private plane for recreation. After hours spent waiting for Kildall to return, and for his wife to sign a non-disclosure agreement (NDA) with IBM—which Gates had earlier signed without hesitation—Sams left Digitial determined to find a more reasonable group of people to do business with. (In fairness, however, there is controversy surrounding what actually occurred on that summer day in 1980; for his part, Kildall maintained that he had been flying his plane back from a business trip, not for recreational purposes.)

Sams contacted Gates, asking him to suggest another operating system besides CP/M. It wasn't just that Sams found Digital's staff to be insufferable; Sams was also worried that the company couldn't produce a version of CP/M for the advanced Intel 8088 in time for the product launch (CP/M had originally been written for the Intel 8080 and Zilog Z80). This time, Paul Allen came to the rescue, recommending that Microsoft contact Tim Paterson of Seattle Computer Products (SCP), which was located near Microsoft headquarters; while SCP was waiting on Digital to produce CP/M for their 16-bit Intel 8086 computer kits, Allen had learned that Paterson had programmed a Quick and Dirty Operating System (QDOS), later known as 86-DOS, which imitated CP/M. Sams gave the go-ahead for Microsoft to purchase the license for 86-DOS and make it fit to IBM's specifications. Gates assigned Paterson the task without telling him anything of the Microsoft-IBM connection; when the work was completed, Microsoft paid SCP $50,000 for exclusive rights to 86-DOS software. (Paterson ultimately left SCP to work for Microsoft.)

Gates remembered the urgency to ship out that first DOS. "But the one that shipped first with the machine and the one that was low priced, because we didn't insist on significant payments, because we wanted it to get out there, was called the IBM Disk Operating System," he said.

> Now, the funny thing is IBM didn't like these acronyms. So, in fact, even the term PC or words like PC DOS, they at first really didn't like people using those. But it became so commonplace that the operating system was sometimes called PC DOS, sometimes called MS-DOS. And, of course, the machine became the PC and all the magazines about it were the PC magazines.

Microsoft was paid more than a half-million dollars by IBM for their work on programming language implementations (BASIC,

FORTRAN, COBOL, and Pascal) as well as the newly christened PC DOS 1.0 for the IBM PC. But Microsoft also received something even more valuable, something that ultimately paved the way for their hegemony in the software world and also permitted Microsoft BASIC to spread to tens of millions of home computers: the permission to sell their DOS—called MS-DOS—to other companies. It was perhaps the business deal of the century. As Walter Isaacson, in his book *The Innovators*, rightly notes, "Gates was gunning for an agreement [with IBM] that would allow Microsoft to keep ownership of an operating system that IBM would turn into a global standard." Unsurprisingly, Kildall never forgave his former friend Gates, claiming that MS-DOS was in effect a carbon copy of CP/M, with aspects like the text-based interface and command prompts being nearly identical. In a concession to Kildall, however, IBM released a version of CP/M, called CP/M-86, on the PC. But the damage was done; whereas less than a decade earlier CP/M was the dominant operating system, something IBM couldn't imagine releasing a personal computer without, now MS-DOS was the standard.

Microsoft made out like a bandit, but so did IBM, at least for a while. The IBM Personal Computer 5150 debuted on August 12, 1981, at the Waldorf Astoria in New York City. The price? Only around fifteen hundred dollars, for a computer capable of color and graphics and ready to host a plethora of peripherals courtesy of expansion slots, such as a monitor, printer, multiple diskette drives, and tons of extra memory (up to 256K); Microsoft BASIC, loaded into ROM, came standard. And in a mass-marketing blitz in print and on television, IBM employed the Charlie Chaplin Little Tramp character to great effect in order to sell the new PC. Modern times indeed.

CHAPTER 12
∞
IBM BASIC Becomes the Standard

The IBM PC rose to the top of the sales charts, with shortages of the product the rule rather than the exception. More significantly, third-party support for the PC also exploded; by 1984, the year the Macintosh was released (to great fanfare and lackluster sales), IBM had the home computer market locked up and the PC had become the standard.

With Microsoft licensing MS-DOS to dozens of other companies, it wasn't long before PC clones—machines that were either entirely compatible with the IBM PC open architecture or nearly so—were flooding the market as well. These reverse-engineered clones, such as from Compaq, were mostly Intel x86-based systems; with the IBM PC BIOS cloned by Phoenix Technologies in 1984, it was easier than ever for companies to assemble hardware and software in a simulacrum of a IBM PC, driving down the prices of all IBM PCs and compatibles while also putting the squeeze on companies like Apple, Atari, Commodore, and even Tandy, who only offered standalone, non-PC compatible machines. (In 1984, *Byte* wrote of tech companies' extreme "drive to be compatible" with the IBM PC. By 1984, Tandy had released the Tandy 1000, its first fully IBM compatible computer; Atari rolled out their PC-1, the first in a series, later in the decade; and Commodore followed suit with their PC-10, which wasn't even backward compatible with their own products. But Apple—which purchased a full-page advertisement in the *Wall Street Journal* that acknowledged IBM's entry into the home computer market with the headline, "Welcome, IBM. Seriously"—never kowtowed to market forces.) And it made all the sense in the world for third-party software makers to fashion games for MS-DOS, since the operating system ran a majority of home computers by the mid-1980s. (Eventually, to retaliate against the clones, IBM ditched MS-DOS in favor of OS/2, which Microsoft coded at the same time it was developing Windows—something IBM had little interest in.)

Of course, with MS-DOS came Microsoft BASIC—specifically, IBM Cassette BASIC (version C1.10) burned into ROM; thus, an operating system was not necessary to run BASIC, since the computer could boot straight to BASIC. As its name implied, IBM Cassette BASIC programs could be saved using the optional cassette interface. When IBM Cassette BASIC loaded up, 62,940 bytes were classified as free; Cassette BASIC lived in 40K of ROM and had a grab bag of graphics functions as well as basic support for peripherals such as the light pen (which permitted a user to draw directly onto the display) and joystick, but no mouse support.

Hot on the heels of IBM Cassette BASIC came IBM Disk BASIC (version D1.10) in 1981; now, floppy disks, instead of cassettes, could be used to save programs. At least 32K of memory was required along with a floppy disk drive, of course. Additional features of Disk BASIC included the ability to call up the current date and time, use of **GET** and **PUT** statements (more about them later on), and access to disk drive(s).

Finally, also in 1981, IBM Advanced BASIC—typically referred to as BASICA (version A1.10)—was released. BASICA, which required 48K of memory as well as a floppy drive, added many additional features—music commands using the built-in speaker, advanced graphics functions, and modem event-handling, as well as external event interrupts—but the interpreter would only run on the IBM PC, not compatibles, because it was loaded directly into ROM. Several versions of BASICA, corresponding with upgraded versions of DOS, were released, each containing subtle differences in the functionality of statements and commands. And a cartridge version of BASICA, containing even more advanced features—e.g., additional graphics capabilities—was exclusively made available for the IBM PCjr, a tailored-for-home-use PC that arrived several years after the original PC. But BASICA still wouldn't work on anything but an IBM—until the Compaq Computer of 1983 came along. *Byte* magazine got their hands on a Compaq prototype. "The systems loaded and executed perfectly," the *Byte* author explained, "with the exception of BASIC on PC-DOS, which wouldn't execute because the Compaq doesn't have ROM BASIC. The BASICA provided on disk and all of the IBM PC sample programs found on the PC-DOS disk ran without incident."

IBM BASIC made use of a tokenizer when storing programs in order to save memory, and programs could be saved as ASCII text files using the **SAVE"PROGRAM",A** command. For example, consider the following "Hello World!" program—the "Hello, World" convention, a simple first program users new to a language should code, is the brainchild of computer scientist Brian Kernighan, author of the book *The C Programming Language*—written in BASICA:

```
10 CLS
20 PRINT"HELLO WORLD!"
30 END
```

Saving a program without the ASCII option—here, by typing **SAVE"HELLO"**—and then opening the program file in a text editor will result in a tokenized, and also strange-looking, format (it's also called a "compressed binary format"):

```
˜t
¿äë"HELLO WORLD!"é-Å
```

Save the program instead as an ASCII file—by typing **SAVE"HELLO",A**—and open the program file in a text editor to see:

```
10 CLS
20 PRINT"HELLO WORLD!"
30 END
```

A "protected" **SAVE** option was also provided, which would save a program in an "encoded binary format"; protected code can be **RUN**, but not **LIST**ed or **EDIT**ed.

Bill Gates claims he was "very involved in the creation of [IBM PC] BASIC." Gates was especially proud of the graphics effects he, Paul Allen, and Neil Konzen were able to coax out of the system's Color Graphics Adapter (CGA) card—a graphics card with 16K of video memory and a maximum of 16 colors available at low resolution. "Neil Konzen and I spent a whole weekend just goofing around with this machine once we had BASIC running and wrote this thing [**CIRCLE.BAS**, where the **.BAS** file extension denotes an IBM BASIC program], **DONKEY.BAS**, **PIECHART.BAS**, these are still shipped today [i.e., at the time of the interview, which was in the early 1990s]. They are kind of obsolete, but they are code that we threw together that weekend."

The sample BASIC programs, along with brief descriptions of each, that came packaged with the very first version of IBM PC DOS in 1981 were as follows:

- **ART.BAS**, many squares and rectangles randomly appear on-screen.
- **BALL.BAS**, an animation of a bouncing ball.
- **CALENDAR.BAS**, prints a wall calendar for any year between 1981 and 1989.
- **CIRCLE.BAS**, a set of quick animations of growing circles and circles-within-circles.
- **COLORBAR.BAS**, a demo of the available colors on-screen.
- **COMM.BAS**, a communication program that allows the computer to interface with a modem.
- **DONKEY.BAS**, an overhead driving game with the objective of avoiding suddenly-appearing donkeys.
- **MORTGAGE.BAS**, calculates mortgage payments, presenting the results in a table format.
- **MUSIC.BAS**, plays a user-selected song.
- **PIECHART.BAS**, creates user-specified pie charts.
- **SAMPLES.BAS**, presents a menu that allows the user run any of the sample programs.
- **SPACE.BAS**, various spaceships appear randomly on-screen.

The sample program **MUSIC.BAS**—which shows a musical keyboard on-screen with available song "selections" such as March, Stars, and Pop—simply linked (technically, **CHAIN**ed) to other BASIC programs (which are not listed above) that played the individual songs.

DONKEY.BAS quickly became notorious, especially at Apple. After the company purchased one of the first IBM PCs, Apple employee Andy Hertzfeld later recalled his first reaction upon playing the game. "The most embarrassing game was a lo-res graphics driving game called 'Donkey,'" he said.

> The player was supposed to be driving a car down a slowly scrolling, poorly rendered "road", and could hit the space bar to toggle the jerky motion.... We thought the concept of the game was as bad as the crude graphics that it used. Since the game was written in BASIC, you could list it out and see how it was written. We were surprised to see that the comments at the top of the game proudly proclaimed the authors: Bill Gates and Neil Konzen.

Hertzfeld was also struck by the fact that IBM PC DOS seemed like a mere "clone" of CP/M, with "the most clunky part of the system [being] the software."

At the ten-year celebration of Visual Basic's release, Gates was asked again about **DONKEY.BAS**. He offered a slightly different recollection:

> Actually, it was myself and Neil Konzen at four in the morning with this prototype IBM PC sitting in this small room. IBM insisted that we had to have a lock on the door and we only had this closet that had a lock on it, so we had to do all our development in there and it was always over 100 degrees, but we wrote late at night a little application to show what the Basic built into the IBM PC could do. And so that was **DONKEY.BAS**. It was at the time very thrilling.

As a joke, at that same ten-year celebration Microsoft unveiled a new version of **DONKEY.BAS**, this time running in three-dimensions, to show off some of the capabilities of their soon-to-be-released VB.NET language.

The code for the original **DONKEY.BAS**, which runs perfectly on BASICA, is suffused with graphics commands that became IBM BASIC standbys: **CLS** (clears the screen), **LINE** (outputs a single line given the coordinates of the endpoints), **PSET** (turns on a pixel), **PRESET** (turns off a pixel), **DRAW** (sketches shapes, using absolute movement or relative movement—by employing a LOGO turtle-like command set), **GET** (captures a rectangular segment of the screen, which is then stored in an array), and **PUT** (displays a stored rectangular segment of the screen). In addition, the **LOCATE** statement, which places text at specified coordinates on-screen, is repeatedly utilized throughout **DONKEY.BAS**. **PEEK** and **POKE** are used several times as well; on line **1170**, for instance, a **PEEK** command ensures that the attached monitor can properly display the game's graphics.

By the mid-1980s, IBM BASIC had become the default, the generic, the standard dialect of the language; whenever the term "BASIC" was uttered, it was assumed to be IBM's. The IBM PC had become *the* Personal Computer, so much so that the term "personal computer" unmoored itself as a proper noun and simply referred to a general class of non-mainframe, non-kit, small and compact microcomputers for individuals, in the same way as "Xeroxing" transformed into a verb for copying paper—on any copy machine, not just a Xerox—and "pass me a Kleenex" became synonymous with the phrase "pass me a tissue," irrespective of the brand. BASIC became, like Xerox and Kleenex, a proprietary eponym; BASIC came to refer to either Microsoft BASICA or GW-BASIC, Microsoft's final line-numbered BASIC interpreter.

CHAPTER 13

∞

The Twilight of Line-Numbered BASIC

In 1983, shortly after Compaq engineered Advanced BASIC to run on their Compaq Computers ROM-free, Microsoft went to work on their own ROM-free version: GW-BASIC.

Debate still swirls around the meaning of the letters "GW" in GW-BASIC. Gregory Whitten, a Harvard-trained mathematician and former chief software architect, was intimately involved with the development of Microsoft BASIC and BASIC in general, with a legacy extending back to 1970. In a publicly posted e-mail from 2005, Whitten's muddled attempts at settling the "GW" debate simply stoked the flames of confusion:

> If GW-BASIC is named for anyone, it is probably me because I developed the Microsoft BASIC language standards in the BASIC Compiler line. The BASIC interpreter was much harder to extend and usually followed afterwards. The other story is that it stands for Gee-Whiz BASIC and it sounded good to the Japanese OEMs [original equipment manufacturers] at the time because it had graphics features added to the language....
>
> The GW-BASIC name stands for Gee-Whiz BASIC. The GW- name was picked by Bill Gates. He is the one who knows whether it was Gee-Whiz or after me because it has been used both ways.

Notwithstanding some features of standalone BASICs produced in the 1970s and early '80s, GW-BASIC is arguably the *ne plus ultra* of Microsoft's family of line-numbered BASICs stretching back to the Altair—and perhaps even of line-numbered BASIC in general. GW-BASIC cobbled together nearly everything in Advanced BASIC—excepting cassette operations, which were unsurprisingly not supported considering the ascendance of floppy disks—but did it as a standalone executable, not dependent on ROM; therefore, GW-BASIC was able to be distributed far and wide, and it was—packaged in MS-DOS, GW-BASIC came pre-installed in a surfeit of IBM clones, ready for users to code to their heart's content right beneath the eternally patient **Ok** prompt.

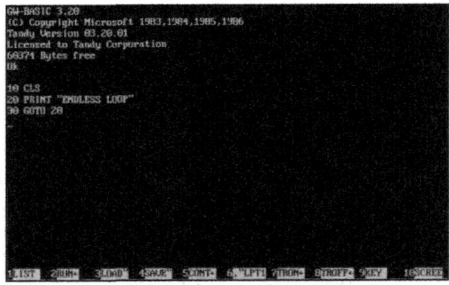

GW-BASIC for the Tandy 1000.

The definitive book on GW-BASIC, *The GW-BASIC Reference* (1990) by Don Inman and Bob Albrecht (who founded the People's Computer Company and also wrote a classic BASIC book in 1972 called *My Computer Likes Me When I Speak in BASIC*), makes no bones about how pervasive and influential GW-BASIC (and BASICA) had become: "Since there are 20 or 30 million copies of GW-BASIC in the hands of computer users, this version of BASIC has become the worldwide standard. Even compiled BASICs, such as Microsoft's QuickBASIC and Spectra Software's PowerBasic, have their roots in GW-BASIC." (Microsoft developed, and IBM released, several compilers for IBM BASIC, all called BASCOM [Basic Compiler], which were precursors to the QuickBASIC compilers. Other BASIC compilers had already been written for the Apple and the TRS-80 by Microsoft. QuickBASIC and PowerBasic are covered in chapter 14.) Interestingly, though their text is by far the most comprehensive work on GW-BASIC ever published, they admit to using Tandy BASIC—which "is also virtually the same as

GW-BASIC, and is bundled with the Tandy 1000 series of computers"—in order to write the book.

Open up a typical type-in cookbook (so-called because of its pages and pages of algorithmic recipes for the user to literally type in, line by line) from the mid-1980s, and you'll find that, indeed, IBM BASIC was the *lingua franca*. To wit: consider *Computer Monsters* (1984) by Stephen Manes and Paul Somerson, a book overflowing with creative, albeit text-based, "scary" and "horror"-type games such as "Monster Memory," whose description reads as follows: "Terrible monsters are coming to get you. There's just one thing they can't stand—humans who remember exactly what they look like. If you've got a monstrous memory, you'll survive. If not... well, don't say we didn't warn you!" Like most type-in cookbooks, *Computer Monsters* is part of a tradition inaugurated with *101 Games in BASIC* by David Ahl. Ahl notes in his book's preface that

> with few exceptions, the games all run in 'standard' BASIC.... The major difference between various computer systems appears to be in the handling of alphabetic strings. On Digital [Equipment Corporation] systems a subscripted string variable, for example, `A$(8)` or `Cl$(15)`, refers to a variable in an array or matrix. Other BASIC compilers may not have string arrays.

Ahl wrote that from his seat at Digital in July of 1973, years before the Microsoft hegemony over BASIC would occur, so presuming people would run BASIC on Digital equipment was as good of an assumption as any then. (Also a good assumption: that programs would be run on a BASIC compiler, rather than an interpreter.) Ahl's programs might just as well have been running on a Teletype.

But the story is different in the "Welcome, Human!" preface to *Computer Monsters*. A question to the reader is posed on page 1: "Will these programs run on my computer?" The authors' answer: "If you have an IBM Personal Computer or IBM PCjr, the answer is YES! All you have to do is type in the Program Listing. You shouldn't need to make any changes at all." (Just to be on the safe side you might want to type `WIDTH 40`, though, if you have a color monitor, to set the printed line width properly. If your computer wasn't producing a 40-column display, words and sentences might be cut off at seemingly random locations, making it difficult to read the output.) But if you own an Apple II; an Apple II Plus; an Apple

IIe; an Atari 400, 800, or XL; a Coleco Adam; a Commodore 64 or VIC-20; a Radio Shack TRS-80 Color Computer; a Texas Instruments 99/4A—well, the answer is: Maybe you will have to make some changes to the programs. After all, there are differences between these computers: some have RETURN keys, while others have ENTER keys; some machines can produce capital letters, while others cannot. Even the way that a user breaks out of a program varies from machine to machine (e.g., on some computers, press the BREAK key; on others, press CTRL BREAK, or press CONTROL C, or press FCTN 4). If you have an Apple II with only Integer BASIC, don't even bother typing the programs in—they won't work (recall Integer BASIC's lack of floating-point capability); only Applesoft will do, and even then, you'll have to make changes, mostly involving **RANDOMIZE** statements (which generate seeds for the pseudorandom number generator). Same with the Commodore, the Color Computer, and the Coleco Adam (released by toy and videogame maker Coleco Industries): **RANDOMIZE** won't work as advertised, and you'll also have to fiddle around with the **RND** function (which generates the pseudorandom numbers). The Coleco has other issues, too, mostly around display characters. The Atari won't permit string arrays, so those will have to be revised, and even string variables will have to be "**DIM**ensioned" (i.e., using the **DIM** statement) prior to use. Worst of all—or, at least, most different from the IBM BASIC de facto standard, depending on your perspective—is Texas Instruments: there are special characters needed for Boolean logic statements, different string-manipulation functions, and unique rules for conditional statements. Interestingly, the functioning of the **RANDOMIZE** statement seems to have been a longstanding issue, well prior to IBM BASIC; Ahl's book cautions readers about it as well: "Many programs use the **RANDOMIZE** command to start the random number generator at a random point. Some BASIC compilers do not recognize **RANDOMIZE** and it must be removed in order for the program to run."

True, the programs of *Computer Monsters* didn't tap into many of the more advanced functions Microsoft had added into IBM BASIC, but the book's programs were also a step above those that ran at Dartmouth in the 1960s on Teletypes. The community of BASIC programmers, for so many years lacking standardized commands for graphics, sound, cursor movement, strings, and the like, was finally beginning to acquiesce to the Microsoft BASIC juggernaut; for example, of the most popular teach-yourself-BASIC books of the time was Donald McCunn's *Computer Programming for the Compleat Idiot for the Apple, Commodore, IBM, TRS-80 and Microsoft BASIC*.

Microsoft BASIC had its own particular, rather mysterious method of generating pseudorandom numbers using the **RND** statement—but not truly *random* numbers, since digits were generated deterministically by using a recursive function that required an initial number seed (which could be user-entered using the **RANDOMIZE** statement, or pulled from the computer's internal clock using the **RANDOMIZE TIMER** statement); a particular seed x would produce the same sequence of pseudorandom numbers every time.

John von Neumann created the first pseudorandom number generator algorithm in the late 1940s; called the middle-square method, it worked like this: start with an n-digit number seed, square the seed, and then take the middle n digits (adding leading digits if necessary to ensure the product has n digits) as the next number in the sequence. IBM BASIC's pseudorandom number generator algorithm is undoubtedly more complicated than the middle-square method. But it's tough to get to the bottom of precisely which recursive function IBM BASIC uses. In "A Theoretical and Empirical Comparison of Mainframe, Microcomputer, and Pocket Calculator Pseudorandom Number Generators," published in a 1993 issue of the academic journal *Behavior Research Methods, Instruments, & Computers*, author Patrick Onghena writes that

> [t]he Advanced BASIC (IBM, 1986), GW-BASIC (Microsoft, 1987), and QBASIC (Microsoft, 1991) programming languages provide the function **RND**, which is initialized by the **RANDOMIZE** command together with a number between -2^{15} and $2^{15}-1$, and which returns a pseudorandom single-precision number between 0 and 1…. [T]he generating algorithm is undocumented in the manual. Our letters to Microsoft Inc. about the algorithm remain unanswered.

When searched for pseudorandom generation, the Microsoft website explains, "Microsoft Basic uses the linear-congruential method [a common pseudorandom number generator algorithm] for random-number generation in the **RND** function," but the "Basic" mentioned probably isn't GW-BASIC, but likely Visual Basic. Thus, the mystery of GW-BASIC random number generation will likely remain just that—a mystery.

Avid consumers of computer culture in the 1980s couldn't avoid type-ins, not just in cookbooks like *Computer Monsters* but in magazines as well. Periodicals like *The Rainbow*, a monthly geared toward the TRS-80 Color Computer; *RUN* magazine, which focused on the Commodore (in 1984, the now famous **10 PRINT** line appeared in the magazine); and *Compute!*, which wasn't platform-specific but had its roots as the Commodore-only *Pet Gazette*, regularly published BASIC type-ins for their readers. (*Compute!* also published *Compute!'s Gazette*, which was proprietary to the Commodore.) Type-ins had a unique appeal in a world where software wasn't a point and a click away. As Harry McCracken, who wrote a lengthy article for *Time* magazine celebrating the fiftieth anniversary of BASIC, explains, "Typing in programs from listings was an intellectual exercise rather than mere rote effort, in part because you often ended up adapting them for your computer's version of Microsoft BASIC." Furthermore, you might be tempted to improve the code; program listings demythologized and deconstructed the software, raising your confidence at writing your own professional-quality programs. "The wiring of these printed and memorized programs was sometimes messed up, but they were not sealed from view in a closed black box," the authors of *10 PRINT* note. The type-in was an educational tool training would-be programmers; of course, the downside was the hours spent keying in code, and the consequent high probability, since every letter and symbol and space had to be in the right place, of making typos—mitigated somewhat, but not completely, by checksum routines like *Compute!*'s Automatic Proofreader, which was a short error-checking algorithm that proofread your typing line-by-line by having you compare sets of "rem" numbers appended to the ends of lines (e.g., ":rem 22"). But plenty of syntax errors were sure to terminate program runs regardless.

Eventually, some BASIC authors began to get more creative and experiment with the type-in format. Instead of simply writing a description of a program, including a sample run, and displaying a source code listing, as David Ahl's books—and their many, many successors and spinoffs (the TRS-80 family alone had dozens of them, as did the Commodore 64 and the Apple II)—did, these authors wrapped fiction stories around their program listings, forcing a reader to engage in the narrative by running the associated type-ins. For instance, Stuart and Donna Paltrowitz wrote a series of *Computer Storybooks* in genres like science fiction, mystery, and adventure. As they explain in the introduction to one of their books,

> Within each story [each chapter] there are computer programs [in BASIC]. You will be asked to type the programs into your computer and then answer some questions. The computer will 'talk back' and respond to your answers. The computer's answers will surprise and amuse you.

In effect, type-in storybooks were leveraging the interactivity of the computer—and the ubiquity of BASIC and the ease of BASIC programming—to enhance print-only gamebooks, works of interactive fiction like the *Choose Your Own Adventure* series. Since most type-in storybooks weren't computer brand-specific, their code listings tended not to make use of hardware-dependent graphics or sound functions but rather were mostly text-based. Stuart and Donna Paltrowitz's *Computer Storybooks* even avoided loops and conditional statements, all in an effort to work as is in as many BASIC dialects as possible.

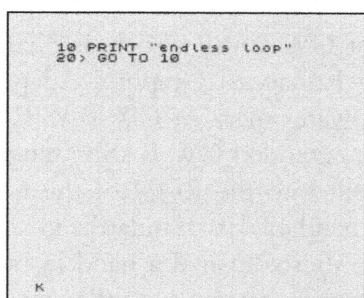

Sinclair BASIC for the Sinclair ZX Spectrum.

Even so, there were still changes that needed to be made, such as for Clive Sinclair's Sinclair ZX Spectrum personal computer, jointly manufactured by the Sinclair and Timex Corporation and popular in Europe in the 1980s. Although Sinclair BASIC, first written for the Sinclair ZX80 in 1979 by Nine Tiles' John Grant (a 4K ROM integer-only version) and then updated in 1980 by Grant's colleague Steve Vickers for the ZX81 (an 8K ROM floating-point version; there was a bug early on that produced an incorrect square root for the decimal 0.25) and the color 16K ROM ZX Spectrum, didn't deviate too much from Microsoft BASIC—there were several notable differences, such as variable names being permitted to be keywords and the IDE catching syntax errors almost in real-time—the means of keyboard entry did differ, with single keystrokes sufficient to enter in full keywords like **LET** and **PRINT**. Also, there was no apostrophe on its very compact keyboard. Other computers popular in Europe, like the Dragon 32/64, were similar enough to popular computers stateside—in the Dragon's case, the TRS-80 Color Computer—as to not even need mentioning in *Computer Storybooks*.

Other type-in storybooks, like the *Micro Adventure* series published by Scholastic, offered even more complex type-ins integrated into long-form narrative. But type-ins declined in popularity by the end of the 1980s—*Compute!* stopped offering them in their pages in 1988, while *The Rainbow* had a late death in 1993—in part because of the ever-increasing complexity of programs (which were not, by and large, being written in BASIC anymore), and also due to the reduced costs of simply including program listings on diskette or even CD-ROM rather than on paper. By that point, though Microsoft BASIC was the de facto standard, GW-BASIC was on its way out, too.

Latter versions of GW-BASIC, such as 3.20, and the final version, 3.23, included Enhanced Graphics Adapter (EGA) support, which was the high-water mark of GW-BASIC's graphics capabilities. Microsoft even extended GW-BASIC tangentially in the form of MSX BASIC, built into the ROM of the MSX Personal Computer yet easily expandable, a standardized computing platform based in Japan that Microsoft had a hand in building. Despite the improvements, however, it was too little, too late: programming had moved on from the clunky blank screen, blinking cursor, command line-based Integrated Development Environment (IDE) that breathlessly waited in anticipation for your line-numbered unstructured code. On the surface, GW-BASIC still looked an awful lot like the Dartmouth Time-Sharing System running Dartmouth

BASIC. But, unlike with those relatively unforgiving BASIC compilers of the 1960s, GW-BASIC's IDE was flexible, with BASIC code as fungible as it would ever be on a line-numbered IDE.

Even the act of line numbering, very much a lost skill, was algorithmic in nature. In the book *Bad Choices: How Algorithms Can Help You Think Smarter and Live Happier* (2017), author Ali Almossawi classifies the "gaps" that BASIC programmers typically left between line numbers—such as 10, 20, 25, 30, 100, and so forth—as an instance of a "library sort" or "gapped-insertion sort" algorithm, which improves the "insertion sort"—in which the addition of one item into a list causes a chain reaction, pushing over every item thereafter—by setting aside pockets of space so that fewer shifts need to take place. "The first language I ever programmed in was BASIC. During a recent conversation with a friend, I was reminded of a memory I had all but forgotten—that line numbers in that programming language typically had 'gaps' between them," recalls Almossawi. "Line two didn't follow line one, rather line twenty might have followed line ten, and so on. That convention allowed a programmer to add new lines in between existing lines while avoiding the drudgery of having to renumber them." It's a space-for-time tradeoff that most BASIC programmers, whether they realized it or not, made. As *10 PRINT* observes, "[Line numbering by 10s] was an acknowledgement that a program is dynamic, rather than fixed and perfect."

GW-BASIC was arguably the most advanced, most dynamic, and most complete realization of unstructured line-numbered BASIC ever made, but by the late 1980s Microsoft had put GW-BASIC out to pasture—by not bundling it with MS-DOS anymore. (There are two good options for still using GW-BASIC on modern operating systems: running the original executable file using the MS-DOS emulator DOSBox, or instead downloading PC-BASIC, a near-perfect language emulator that "aims for bug-for-bug compatibility with Microsoft GW-BASIC," programmed in Python by Rob Hagemans.) Microsoft did, however, include a (somewhat) new version of BASIC in MS-DOS called QBASIC, which offered an alternative approach to programming in the language.

CHAPTER 14

∞

BASIC Gets Structured

QBASIC was born from the ashes of GW-BASIC, offering programmers a newly structured version of an old language.

By the early 1980s, BASIC was ubiquitous in American middle and high schools, with microcomputers such as the TRS-80 and the Apple II booting straight to the computer language, forcing students to navigate their way around these computers using BASIC commands. BASIC shielded its users from the goings-on inside their computers; students weren't required to master the mnemonics of assembly or the complexities and nuance of FORTRAN to compel their computers to do something useful. BASIC was a user-friendly language, the barrier to entry into the world of computer programming low, with very little in the way of writing a small, intuitive, ready-to-execute program: write a two-line program like the one shown below, run it, and the output appears immediately on the display (or, earlier, the Teletype):

```
10 PRINT "TIME FLIES LIKE AN ARROW"
20 PRINT "FRUIT FLIES LIKE A BANANA"
RUN

TIME FLIES LIKE AN ARROW
FRUIT FLIES LIKE A BANANA

READY
```

But with this sandbox-like freedom came a downside: lack of structure. Other programming languages, which were by the 1980s being taught en masse in universities—not to mention being used in industry and academic environments—weren't different from BASIC in terms of the degree, they were different in kind, requiring users to code in a structured manner. One of those languages was Pascal.

Pascal was created by Niklaus Wirth, who named the language after the seventeenth century French mathematician Blaise Pascal. Wirth built Pascal off of ALGOL, one of the original high-level programming languages. ALGOL was designed by a committee in Zurich in the 1950s to be platform independent, namely, to have a universal syntax and structure. Consequently, ALGOL never achieved even a fraction of the popularity of FORTRAN because implementations of the language, unlike the language itself, could not be consistent—they had to be machine dependent, compilers written in different machine languages for each implementation.

The Swiss computer scientist Niklaus Wirth, who had been part of the committee tasked with creating ALGOL, published an extension of that language, called Pascal, in 1970. Pascal offered a number of advantages over ALGOL, including type checking (a type system that makes sure that variable-use rules are enforced; mixing types, like real numbers and integers, could lead to errors), malleability with data types (such as subrange types, which restrict the values variables can assume, and complex types, built off of other types of variables), shedding symbols in favor of English-style keywords, and easier platform implementation of compilers through an intermediate system called Pascal-P.

To address a growing need for early computer literacy, in 1984 the Educational Testing Service (ETS) adopted Pascal as its language of choice for testing high school students for college credit in Advanced Placement (AP) Computer Science. ETS chose Pascal, rather than FORTRAN or BASIC, because of Pascal's structured and strongly-typed approach along with its burgeoning popularity and growing respect among academics; students majoring in computer science were going to learn Pascal anyway, so why not expose them to an AP subset of the language while they were still in high school? This feedback loop, along with well-designed multi-platform implementations (such as from Borland), made Pascal the language of choice for educators by the 1990s. (ETS eventually dumped Pascal in favor of a subset of C++ and then Java; regardless, Kurtz has called AP CS courses "much too complicated." If Kurtz had his way, he would teach introductory CS courses with a structured form of BASIC. Teaching Java to young kids is "nuts. It's just nuts," Kurtz said, especially take umbrage at the language's punctuation rules, comparing them unfavorably with FORTRAN's.)

Educational theorists were sounding the alarm against teaching BASIC to students almost from BASIC's birth. For example, in the 1971 article "Science Teaching and Computer Languages," author Alfred M. Bork offers a telling (and soon to be considered representative) anecdote about students learning BASIC:

> ... I have had several examples recently of good students, brought up on BASIC in [their schools], who have had psychological problems in switching from BASIC to a more powerful language. This experience may represent a chance occurrence, or it may be a phenomenon observable for all languages. As experience develops with languages, we should keep close contact with "changeability." A person can become accustomed to a language so that it is a "pacifier" to the user, a retreat in moments of crisis.

Bork was especially aghast at BASIC's casualness with subroutines. "The ability to conceptualize a large problem as a series of solvable subproblems, making little problems out of a big problem," is critical, he writes. But "BASIC is perhaps the weakest in this regard, as subroutines are possible only by in-line coding in most forms of BASIC in current use; this seems pedagogically unsatisfactory." That BASIC was weak with subroutines is no accident; from the earliest implementations of Dartmouth BASIC, Kemeny and Kurtz admit that they only provided the **GOSUB/RETURN** keywords for subroutines "grudgingly," pointedly calling a subroutine an "avoidable" "luxury item" in the BASIC the First user manual. Since those early implementations of BASIC couldn't truly compartmentalize subroutines—namely, subroutines couldn't be named or addressed with anything other than a line number, and all variables initialized within a program were automatically of global scope, never local—structured coding was very difficult. Only by BASIC the Sixth did true subroutines, formally called "subprograms," come into being; but by then earlier Dartmouth BASIC implementations had already proliferated outside of Dartmouth, leaving the benefits of this stable structured version stuck on campus.

Seymour A. Papert, an advocate of early computer use in schools and intimately involved with the creation of the LOGO programming language, compares in his book *Mindstorms: Children, Computers, and Powerful Ideas* (1980) the default educational use of BASIC to the reliance on the QWERTY keyboard arrangement, arguing that both BASIC's and QWERTY's reasons for dominance weren't rational, but merely historical. When computers were limited in memory and speed—not to mention expensive—the use of BASIC was legitimate, since BASIC was relatively undemanding of the available hardware. Yet despite the growing ubiquity of cheap computers, Papert notes that

> ... in most high schools, [BASIC] remains almost synonymous with programming, despite the existence of other computer languages that are demonstrably easier to learn and are richer in the intellectual benefits that can come from learning them. The situation is paradoxical. The computer revolution has scarcely begun, but is already breeding its own conservatism.
>
> ... [P]eople invent "rationalizations" to justify the status quo. In the case of BASIC, the phenomenon has gone much further, to the point where it resembles ideology formation. Complex arguments are invented to justify features of BASIC that were originally included because the primitive technology demanded them or because alternatives were not well enough known at the time the language was designed.

One of these rationalizations, Papert says, is that since most implementations of BASIC have so few keywords, BASIC is an easy language to learn. But just because a particular language—computer or otherwise—has few words doesn't necessarily imply that it is easy to pick up or master. Expecting students to be able to successfully navigate their way around computers by only learning BASIC, Papert explains, is akin to exposing children only to pidgin English translations of poetry and still expecting them to appreciate the range, substance, breadth, and meaning of the embedded ideas.

Even more trenchant criticisms of BASIC are relayed in the article "Programming Language Choice: A Positive Albeit Ambiguous Case for BASIC Programming in Secondary Science Teaching"

(1986) by William W. Cobern. BASIC doesn't require a structured programming style, so "most students approach BASIC programming solutions to a problem with little forethought or planning. They program on a 'stream of conscious' basis. As the programs lengthen, the lack of planning usually results in... spaghetti code," he explains, because if you print out students' code and trace a line from each use of GOTO to its associated line number, the resulting mess of lines on the paper might very well resemble a bowl of spaghetti. (Cobern also notes that unlike BASIC, Pascal "demands structure" and therefore might indeed be a better option for secondary students.)

Spaghetti code was aided and abetted by the frequent use of the GOTO statement, which performed an unconditional jump from any line number to any other line number in a program—thus frequently making code effectively unreadable, since tracing the path the interpreter took through a program could conceivably have countless twists and turns. GOTO was the last refuge of the newbie programmer, and the influential computer scientist Edsger W. Dijkstra found the practice deplorable. In the piece "Go To Statement Considered Harmful" (1968), he bluntly states, "For a number of years I have been familiar with the observation that the quality of programmers is a decreasing function of the density of go to statements in the programs they produce." GOTO is superfluous and should be eliminated (except in machine language), he writes, since "[t]he go to statement as it stands is just too primitive; it is too much an invitation to make a mess of one's program." Use GOTO indiscriminately—in any programming language that made it available, such as BASIC or FORTRAN—and an endless loop might be the result.

Most famously, and devastatingly, comes Dijkstra's criticism of the BASIC language in "How Do We Tell Truths that Might Hurt?" (1975). After presenting his discomfort with the state of affairs in computing, Dijkstra poses a question: "Is not our prolonged silence fretting away Computing Science's intellectual integrity?" Answering in the affirmative, he proceeds to list some "unpleasant truths," mostly having to do with a variety of programming languages. One of those truths is that

> It is practically impossible to teach good programming to students that have had a prior exposure to BASIC: as potential programmers they are mentally mutilated beyond hope of regeneration.

"Mentally mutilated beyond hope of regeneration"—well, that's quite a bit worse than the "psychological problems" caused by BASIC that Alfred M. Bork documented.

But elsewhere Dijkstra deployed an elitist streak when it came to computer programming in general: only the absolute best, most talented programmers need apply, and the rest can just go do something else. Programming was not for everybody. The idea of a language like BASIC, expressly designed for the proletariat, was no doubt antithetical to Dijkstra's worldview. Harry McCracken's piece in *Time* quotes Thomas Kurtz's reaction to the criticism that BASIC wasn't an appropriate way to learn computer programming: "I'll go out on a limb and suggest the degrading of BASIC by the professionals was just a little bit of jealousy—after all, it took years for us to develop our skill; how is it that complete idiots can write programs with just a few hours of skill?"

There were some BASIC defenders, such as experimental psychologist Eugene Galanter in *Kids and Computers* (1983): "BASIC lets you write programs the way Mozart wrote music, by improvising as you go along," meaning that the planning for the program and the programming itself can often occur simultaneously, almost dialectically, at the expense of rigorous preplanning. In *The Computing Teacher* article "When Children Learn Programming: Antecedents, Concepts and Outcomes" (1985), Ben Shneiderman conducted studies confirming that BASIC programming structures were more user-friendly than other languages'. An article in *Compute!* described the state of BASIC affairs by the 1980s:

> Critics of BASIC often decry its lack of structure—it's not only possible, but quite easy, to write a BASIC program so disorganized that even the programmer cannot easily decipher it. On the other hand, BASIC's freedom from excessive structure-promoting rules is the very feature which attracts many programmers who prefer a more freeform style. Structured languages tend to encourage the production of more readable code, but also tend to impose more rules on the programmer. The de-

bate over how rigidly structured a programming language should be is unlikely to end anytime soon.

So, a pitched battle, decades in the making, ensued: the hardscrabble, language-for-the-masses BASIC against the world of "respectable" programming. BASIC was positioned as a kind of status quo goliath, and its advocates' voices were drowned out by the mass of critics, carrying their torches and pitchforks, demanding a quick end to the hegemony of loosely procedural, unstructured BASIC.

Yet the teach-yourself-unstructured-BASIC books were still selling by the tens of thousands. As *10 PRINT* notes, "BASIC was so canonical [through the late 1970s into the 1980s] that some books of BASIC programs did not even bother to mention 'BASIC' on their covers." One such example *10 PRINT* mentions is the popular *What to Do After You Hit Return* by Bob Albrecht: "Not once did the acronym BASIC appear on the front or back cover, perhaps indicating that the language was so prevalent for recreational programming that it need not be named." The award-winning children's science writer Seymour Simon penned an especially popular, prodigiously illustrated introductory programming book which did, however, mention BASIC on the cover; entitled *The BASIC Book*, it was only 32 breezy pages and perfect for the elementary school student; in it, Simon discusses several examples of simple linenumbered programs written in generic BASIC, carefully explaining keywords such as **GOTO**. *The BASIC Book* was published in 1985.

Despite the enduring popularity of line-numbered BASIC, Microsoft realized that the tide was turning. Taking a cue from Pascal, Microsoft reshaped GW-BASIC in 1985, stripping away line numbers while reshaping the language to allow for a structured, procedure-oriented programming style; true subroutines (called subprocedures) became available, and variable declaration and user-defined types were added, among other improvements. This revamped, modernized, and streamlined BASIC was named QuickBASIC, but it was not free nor did it come packaged with an operating system.

But QuickBASIC wasn't Microsoft's first foray into structured BASIC. When the company released Macintosh BASIC in 1984 (putting MacBASIC out to pasture) and AmigaBASIC in 1985 (superseding MetaComCo's ABasiC, which shipped with the earliest

Commodore Amiga operating systems), which were both very similar implantations, the rudiments of structured programming had already taken hold: line numbers were optional while English-style labels (for unconditional jumps) were permitted. Plus, the IDE had advanced: there were now separately designated regions on-screen in which to code, run programs, and utilize programming tools.

The first QuickBASIC compiler was released in August of 1985; soon after, an IDE was packaged with the compiler, along with a full-fledged interpreter as well as additional improvements in control structures. But by 1991, Microsoft also realized that a free replacement for GW-BASIC was needed—after all, programming in Microsoft BASIC had more or less remained relatively unchanged since the days of the Altair—and the company stumbled upon an obvious solution: QuickBASIC, specifically the 1988 (but not the last) iteration, version 4.5. But not the entire software package; the QuickBASIC compiler and linker were excised, along with a few other features. The result was called QBASIC (the "Q" stood for "Quick") version 1.0, containing an interpreter and IDE, which came packaged with MS-DOS 5.0 and later as well as several iterations of Windows. GW-BASIC/BASICA was no longer bundled with MS-DOS.

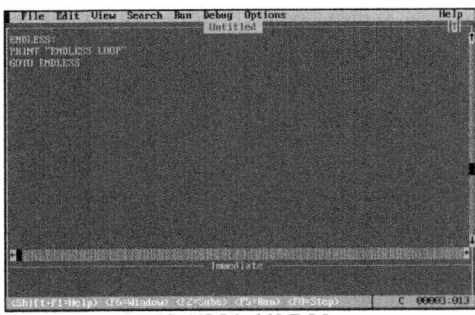
QBASIC for MS-DOS.

QBASIC, like the very first version of IBM PC DOS in 1981, had sample programs. There was **REMLINE.BAS**, a utility that removed line numbers from old BASIC programs; **MONEY.BAS**, a personal finance manager; **NIBBLES.BAS**, a version of the arcade game *Snake* where the "snake" and the "pellets," which are integers, are all fashioned out of ASCII characters; and **GORILLA.BAS**, one of the strangest games ever distributed by Microsoft (although, admittedly, it has some stiff competition, considering games like **DONKEY.BAS**). *Gorillas* is a variant of the ballistic artillery game. In *Gorillas*, two gorillas stand perched atop skyscrapers with an infinite supply of explosive bananas. The objective? By inputting an accurate angle and velocity, throw an explosive banana so precisely that it hits the other gorilla—and watch the surviving gorilla launch into a bizarre celebration routine. Since the source code of *Gorillas*, which used many graphics functions, could be examined and tinkered with in the QBASIC IDE, the game served as an effective QBASIC instructional tool.

The QBASIC IDE is clean and well designed, with dropdown menus located at the top of the screen for loading and saving programs, copying and pasting text within the code, initializing functions and subroutines, finding and replacing text within the code, viewing subroutines and the body of programs in a split screen (or shifting to the output window), starting or continuing a particular program run, debugging programs dynamically, and selecting options (such as changing the colors of the display). Furthermore, when coding in the IDE's "program mode," clicking the "immediate mode"—located in a panel at the bottom of the screen—executes commands immediately (immediate mode roughly correlates to the direct mode of statement entry in GW-BASIC). The cursor can quickly move and edit code anywhere on-screen in a way reminiscent of the Commodore 64's BASIC IDE, albeit with mouse control. The QBASIC interface is leaps and bounds more functional than the menu-less empty screen, blinking cursor, command line-based IDE of old, but it is also not so intimidating as to scare off the neophyte.

Error checking improved immeasurably with QBASIC. Run a program (by pressing the F5 key) and if there's a syntax error, the program will terminate and highlight the location of the error in the code. Breakpoints could be turned on or off, and the "Trace" feature would toggle back and forth between the output window and the program mode.

Line numbers are optional in QBASIC—and never necessary. Instead, whenever a conditional or unconditional jump (the **GOTO** statement is still permitted) is required, a program label has to be created. For example, the following code queries the user for a positive number. If a negative number is entered, that number is discarded in favor of a new number—this time positive—that the user must enter (ad infinitum, if the user insists on being stubborn):

```
ENTRY:
PRINT "Enter a positive number: "
INPUT Num
IF Num < 0 THEN GOTO ENTRY
PRINT "You entered the number "; Num
```

The label in the program above is called **ENTRY** and, like all program labels, is followed by a colon (:). Spaghetti code is still possible but less likely in QBASIC than GW-BASIC, since instead of there being addresses on every line—i.e., in the form of line numbers—such addresses (labels) must now be purposefully inserted throughout the code before unconditional jumps can take effect. (Of course, eliminating the **GOTO** statement altogether would have significantly decreased the probability of encountering a QBASIC program with spaghetti code, but it would also have rendered QBASIC effectively incompatible with GW-BASIC.)

Most GW-BASIC programs were compatible as is with QBASIC, meaning a GW-BASIC program could be loaded and run in QBASIC with a good chance of working properly without any changes; for example, QBASIC left in place

- the unconditional jumps in the form of **GOTO**, **GOSUB**, and **RETURN**;
- the non-zero-based index numbering of arrays of the BASICs of old;
- the option to use the **LET** keyword for variable assignment;
- the extensive mathematical and string functions;
- most of the graphics functions, including the **PUT** and **GET** statements for working with sprites;
- the commands for reading from and writing to files;
- the panoply of types of variables, but QBASIC added a formal declaration statement that allowed for the "shedding" of a type character appended to the variable—though variable declaration was optional. Now, instead of initializing a string variable this way, as was done in GW-BASIC:

```
10 NAME$="GATES"
```

In QBASIC, a string variable could be declared and then initialized with no dollar sign ($) necessary:

```
DIM N AS STRING
N = "GATES"
```

Besides with strings, in QBASIC integers, long-integers, and single- and double-precision variables could also be declared and initialized without any need for the type characters of GW-BASIC (the % for integers, ! for single-precision, and # for double-precision variables).

But similarities between GW-BASIC and QBASIC also implied that the old unstructured style of BASIC programming was still processable by QBASIC for users not yet comfortable or familiar with the structured programming style that languages like Pascal were making commonplace.

Writing programs in a structured, procedure-oriented style meant forgoing ad hoc haphazard unconditional jumps in favor of block structures, subroutines and functions, finite **FOR** loops, and conditional jumps. When users were ready to exploit the structured programming aspects of QBASIC, they would encounter these improvements (besides no required line numbers and a flexible IDE):

- Besides the unconditional jumps to labels, the **DO...LOOP**, **IF...THEN**, **FOR...NEXT**, **SELECT CASE**, and **DO...WHILE** statements group blocks of code together;
- Subroutines, called sub-procedures (**SUB**s) in QBASIC, are self-contained blocks of code. In previous versions of Microsoft BASIC, "subroutines" were only informally and nominally so, since code could not be cordoned off from the rest of a program, with all variables being automatically global in scope without exception (i.e., variables could be accessed and modified anywhere within a program). Pre-QBASIC, there was no need to pass a subroutine a variable's value, because all variables were visible everywhere. Not so in QBASIC, where sub-procedures can take param-

eters, and all variables created inside sub-procedures are local in scope (i.e., are only accessible within the sub-procedure), while variables not passed from the main module to the sub-procedure are by default inaccessible within the sub-procedure—although by explicitly using the **SHARED** keyword inside the sub-procedure a variable once only accessible within the main module turns global. Consider the following sub-procedure, which takes one argument:

```
SUB Cnt (Value)
  Value = Value + 1
  PRINT Value
END SUB
```

In the main module, the line

```
Cnt 6
```

will output the number 7, since 6 was passed as an argument to the sub-procedure **Cnt**—a subroutine whose only purpose is to increment the passed value by one unit and print this number on the screen;
- Functions are similar to sub-procedures, but they require at least one parameter and they must return a value back to the main module.

In computer programming, a recursive routine is a procedure or subroutine or function that calls itself; essentially, the next output depends on the previous input. It is, in theory, possible to transform any algorithm that has an iterative structure (i.e., loops) into a recursive one. It is exceptionally difficult to write true recursive code in first-generation unstructured dialects of BASIC, since a "terminating condition" (or "base case"), which is needed to prevent a recursive routine from spinning out of control, cannot be set without having access to local variables. But an issue of *Compute!* magazine from 1982 lays out a possible means of writing recursive code with unstructured BASIC using a first in, first out (FIFO) stack approach in order to solve the Towers of Brahma (Hanoi) puzzle:

The computer must be able to remember "return addresses".... So, before **GOSUB**bing, the "address" to **RETURN** to is put on the computer's stack and later pulled off the stack by **RETURN**. There is a limit to how many return addresses can be pushed on the stack. This is normally no problem since most subroutines go right back via **RETURN**, relieving the stack of the address number. Recursive, self-calling subroutines, however, aren't **RE-TURN**ing. It's **GOSUB-GOSUB-GOSUB**, etc. Unless the recursion is carefully managed, the stack could quickly fill with return addresses and is then said to overflow.

Needless to say, programming in this side-stepping, indirect way is an unnatural mess. But because some variables, such as those in sub-procedures, are local in scope, QBASIC (and QuickBASIC)—like Pascal and other structured languages—is more than capable of running truly recursive routines quickly and easily.

Let's take a look at an example recursive function in QBASIC for generating factorials. In mathematics, a factorial, denoted by a positive integer followed by an exclamation point (!), is the product of some whole number and all whole numbers below it; for instance, 5! is equal to 5×4×3×2×1, or 120. We can code a factorial function recursively in QBASIC as follows:

```
FUNCTION Fact (n)
  IF n = 0 THEN
    Fact = 1
  ELSE
    Fact = n * Fact(n - 1)
  END IF
END FUNCTION
```

Notice the terminating condition (or base case) in the code: if the variable **n** equals **0**, then the **Fact** function returns **1**.

Call the function **Fact** in immediate mode by typing

```
? Fact(5)
```

and the output screen shows 120.

Microsoft no longer included QBASIC in Windows starting with Windows 2000, when DOS was effectively ditched. Picking up the slack, and continuing the QBASIC tradition on a variety of modern hardware and operating systems, is QB64, a standalone BASIC compiler (written in BASIC) that is entirely compatible with old QBASIC code but extends the language. Microsoft was not involved with QB64's design or development. The impetus for QB64 was explained in a 2008 developer interview in the defunct BASIC-only online magazine *Pcopy!* (the magazine's title is a reference to a BASIC graphics statement that copies the contents of one screen to another). "I feel that more modern versions of BASIC (like Visual Basic) are far too complex for beginners," explained Rob (the developer; his nickname is Galleon). "VB confronts you with a zillion options and it can be difficult for new programmers to understand how to get the toolbar-selected objects to interact with each other. There are of course, many derivatives of BASIC each with a particular focus. QB64's focus is on QBASIC compatibility and extending this capability." (Those wishing to run the original QBASIC executable file should download the MS-DOS emulator DOSBox.)

Perhaps unsurprisingly, the proliferation of BASIC dialects continued with the structured, procedure-oriented generation of BASIC programming; though QBASIC was the most popular, due to receiving free distribution in MS-DOS and early versions of Windows, it was not the only such structured BASIC implementation. Another especially popular one was Borland Turbo Basic, which later became PowerBASIC. Turbo Basic has its roots in BASIC/Z, a compiler written by Robert S. Zale, an iconoclastic entrepreneur and all-around Renaissance man who owned and ran music stores and an insurance agency while teaching himself assembly language on the side. Zale wrote BASIC/Z in the mid-1980s, which caught Borland's interest; Borland brought Zale onboard to create Turbo Basic for the company. By the late 1980s, though, Borland discontinued the product, prompting Zale to purchase the rights to Turbo Basic. He changed its name to PowerBASIC, updating the compiler through the years to work with ever-evolving operating systems.

Over in Great Britain, there was Acorn Computers' BBC Microcomputer System (the BBC Micro), an early 1980s 8-bit computer that succeeded the Acorn Atom home computer. The BBC Micro had a MOS Technology 6502 with BBC BASIC stored in ROM. BBC BASIC was written for a television show. The British Broadcasting Corporation (BBC) had created a show centered on computer programming and needed a computer—and a programming language—to fill it out. A system running Microsoft BASIC was dismissed as not being up to par for their audience, so the BBC shopped around, considering Dragon, but ultimately teaming up with Acorn. Acorn already was deep into developing the Proton, which would succeed the Atom computer. The BBC liked the Proton, and, after working with Acorn to make the Proton's BASIC (an evolution of Acorn BASIC) more understandable, more like English, and more structured, the Proton was renamed the BBC Micro and made its debut on *The Computer Programme* show in January 1982. The computer was an instant hit; schools in Britain raced to pack their computer labs with BBC Micros, with children countrywide learning the Microsoft-free dialect of BASIC. BBC BASIC was ported to the IBM PC in 1986 and Windows in 2001, but the language never gained a foothold in the U.S. and didn't gain much traction in the rest of Europe, either.

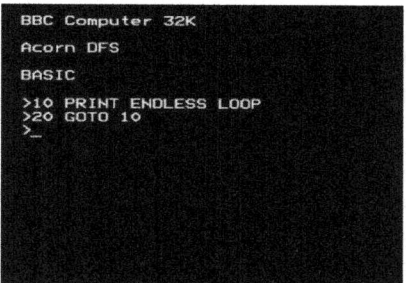

BBC BASIC for the BBC Micro.

SuperBASIC is another structured BASIC dialect to emerge from Britain. Sinclair Research, the British electronics company that released the ZX Spectrum in the early 1980s, had grand plans to release a SuperSpectrum computer. In addition to upgraded hardware and peripherals, the computer would also have a new version of BASIC in tow developed by the software engineer Janice Rosemary Jones. She had been recruited by Oxford physics graduate and self-taught coder Tony Tebby to bring some of the same procedure-based structure present in BBC BASIC to SuperBASIC. Despite the SuperSpectrum project collapsing, SuperBASIC was included in the ROM of Sinclair's next computer: the 1984 upmarket Sinclair QL (Quantum Leap), of which Tebby designed the operating system called QDOS. But QDOS had special routines to integrate it with SuperBASIC, which Tebby later said was "a terrible mistake [that] compromised the OS' integrity." The QL was discontinued two years later, Jones left Sinclair and became an award-winning novelist (under the pen name Jan Jones), and SuperBASIC still has its fans today.

The mid-1980s also saw the emergence of Locomotive BASIC, which came built into the ROM of the British Amstrad CPC (Colour Personal Computer) series of computers. Amstrad, an electronics company, was founded by Alan Sugar, who up until the early 1980s hadn't shown much interest in computers. But then Sugar saw the success of the ZX Spectrum and changed his mind. "We needed to move on and find another sector or product to bring us back to profit growth," he wrote in his autobiography (quoted in the article "You're NOT fired: The story of Amstrad's amazing CPC 464" by Tony Smith). The company began developing the computer in 1983, which would have a monitor, keyboard, and cassette interface yet still be relatively inexpensive. Development of the product started out disastrously. At first, the 6502 processor was chosen to run the machine, but it proved to be too much to handle: the leader of the team, Paul Kelly, walked out on the project.

A new development team was chosen, consisting of childhood friends Roland Perry and William Poel who were very involved in the computer business. Perry had a number of contacts he thought might help Amstrad finish the machine. "I knew a lot of people working in this stuff, and I knew exactly what was necessary in terms of the components," he remembered. "[Y]ou need a Basic interpreter, you need a sound generator, you need a certain resolution on the screen. A lot of computers could only do four colours at a limited resolution, and I wanted to do better than that." Perry drove around England, whipping out the Amstrad's keyboard and cassette player and asking contact after contact he had in the computer and electronics business how they might go about building the rest of the machine. Perry received great advice from a friend at Acorn, who told him to contact Locomotive Software. Arriving at Locomotive as the representative of an unnamed "big British company" while trying to hide Amstrad's intentions, the Amstrad logo on the keyboard case was replaced with the word "Arnold," an anagram of Perry's first name, Roland. At the time of Perry's visit, Locomotive had almost finished Mallard BASIC for the BBC Micro Z80 Second Processor (an expansion unit for the computer), a

Business Basic interpreter built for speed and thus named for the fastest steam-powered locomotive in the world, the London and North Eastern Railway 4468 *Mallard*. Acorn had chosen Locomotive over Microsoft to write the interpreter for the Z80 for two reasons: lower costs and a promise of coding of an indexed file system so that database software was unnecessary.

Amstrad was impressed with Locomotive, so they contracted the company to build a BASIC interpreter for the CPC. Mallard BASIC had been coded in Z80 assembly. Although Locomotive said that they could rewrite Mallard for the 6502 processor, they nonetheless encouraged Amstrad to simply go with the Z80 for the CPC; after all, deadlines were fast approaching, and Locomotive could quickly supply Amstrad with an improved version of Mallard BASIC geared toward personal entertainment rather than business.

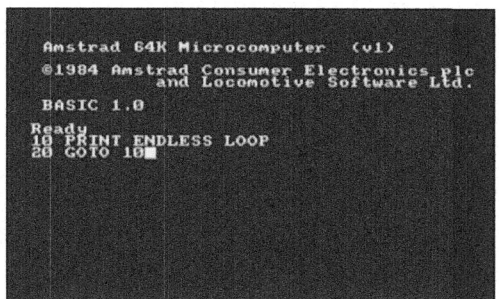
Locomotive BASIC for the Amstrad CPC.

Thus, several months later, Locomotive BASIC was burned into the Amstrad CPC's ROM: half of the memory was used for the original Mallard BASIC, and the other half for the CPC-only improvements. Locomotive BASIC had a rich set of graphics and sound commands easily accessible via keywords (yet kept separate from the firmware, so that even other high-level computer languages could access those same multimedia features with users not having to interact directly with the hardware)—including the ability to work with a maximum of eight windows as well as multi-channel stereo audio—but was lacking some standard structured programming features of the era (e.g., line numbers were required). Especially powerful were the interpreter's **EVERY** and **AFTER** software interrupt controls, permitting subroutines to be called at specially timed intervals. Regardless, the CPC was dead by 1990, but Mallard BASIC, running on the CP/M Plus operating system, lived on for many more years in the Z80 Amstrad PCW line of personal computers.

Back in the United States, however, Kemeny and Kurtz were hard at work on a new BASIC of their own.

CHAPTER 15

∞

Kemeny and Kurtz Strike Back

Disgusted by the many BASIC dialects that had proliferated, in 1983 John Kemeny and Thomas Kurtz decided to go back to the drawing board; within several years they had released a new ANSI-compliant, multiplatform structured BASIC called True BASIC.

With Dartmouth BASIC released into the public domain to encourage widespread acceptance, its creators lost control of the language—a language that Kurtz, recall, had initially thought wouldn't be adopted outside of Dartmouth College. In their underestimation of its popularity, Kemeny and Kurtz failed to get ahead of the problem of standardization, thus leading to the proliferation of innumerable BASIC dialects, some of which stripped down the language, others of which inserted hardware-dependent keywords and functions. (Ironically, Kemeny and Kurtz also relied on a hardware-dependent feature so that they wouldn't have to write floating-point algorithms for BASIC the First: the GE-225's built-in floating-point routines, a key reason why they went with GE in the first place.)

"The implementation of the language is separate from the design of the language," Kurtz explained. Kemeny and Kurtz adopted the vile term "Street BASIC" to speak of the many "inferior" BASIC implementations that proliferated outside the cozy confines of Dartmouth College. "We are greatly concerned that a generation of students is growing up learning Street BASIC, an illiterate dialect of a lovely language," they wrote. The creators had some minor criticisms, like that indentation of code wasn't possible on many Street BASICs. Indentation was purely for "pretty-printing," or aesthetic, reasons: it permitted more readable and understandable code; even by the mid-1960s, Kemeny and Kurtz were promoting its use at Dartmouth.

But they had a number of major criticisms of Street BASIC, too. For one thing, most implementations were interpreters, not compilers (all versions of Dartmouth BASIC were compiled). Interpreters execute only one line of code at a time, only looking for syntax errors, and may fail to recognize missing keywords or more subtle errors of logic in the code or may flag lines that don't actually contain errors. Plus, Street BASIC error-reporting was frequently ugly and non-specific—recall Tiny BASIC's **HOW?**, **WHAT?**, and **SORRY** error messages—making the BASIC language more difficult to use than necessary.

In the interests of saving space, Street BASIC programmers were encouraged to reduce the numbers of spaces (unlike Dartmouth BASIC, these variants tended not to be space-independent), refrain from commenting code, and even change the language itself—by making the **LET** and **END** keywords optional (and thus superfluous) or by completely dropping the **MAT** keyword. Of course, such changes were entirely antithetical to Kemeny and Kurtz's original vision of BASIC: one statement per line, each line beginning with a statement, with a keyword specially designated to declaring the end of a program, and continued encouragement for programmers to write clear, concise, indented, and commented code, while being able to use lowercase characters if possible (the TRS-80 Color Computer, which lacked lowercase, used reverse-video characters to compensate).

Kememy and Kurtz also, unsurprisingly, had a bone to pick with hardware-dependent graphics commands in some BASIC dialects; IBM BASICA/GW-BASIC came under special scrutiny. Instead of conforming to the Cartesian plane (the x-y axis), "[e]vidently, IBM [in reality, Microsoft] chose to follow the television industry, which scans a TV picture starting at the top, rather than us mathematicians, who prefer to use the Cartesian plane we all learned in high school," they wrote. So, to paraphrase Willy Wonka, mathematically converting your monitor's pixel locations to Cartesian coordinate geometry required you to think sideways and slantways and longways and backways and squareways and front ways. Which makes no sense: "If you feel that you need a computer to do all these messy calculations, we agree with you.... But you have a computer! So why does BASICA make you do all the terrible arithmetic? Because it is a very poorly designed language." To be fair, though, it wasn't only BASICA/GW-BASIC that adopted the television industry's standard of the origin at the top left of the screen; most other programming languages adopted the same standard for graphics.

Kemeny and Kurtz had already shown, years before via SBASIC (Structured BASIC), that a structured approach to BASIC was not only possible but preferable. Advanced conditional and looping structures, labeled self-contained subroutines and cases, whitespace, indenting, dropping line numbers altogether, and avoiding unconditional jump constructions (i.e., **GOTO**) are some of the many advantages over its predecessors that a structured form of BASIC brought to the table. In fact, one of the few regrets that Kemeny and Kurtz have publicly expressed with Dartmouth BASIC centers on line numbers: not that they were used per se, but that they served as labels (or addresses) to particular segments of code; if a program needed renumbering, the jumps (**GOTO, GOSUB**, etc.) would need adjusting, too, which was quite a hassle on a command-line IDE. (Although not in IBM BASICA/GW-BASIC; the **RENUM** command adjusted the code accordingly.)

With these ideas in mind, Kemeny and Kurtz got to work on True BASIC, their attempt at a standardized, platform-independent structured BASIC that conformed to many of the original principles of Dartmouth BASIC. Line numbers were vestigial and now optional; **GOTO** wasn't banned but would only work with line numbers. Instead, True BASIC programmers were encouraged to group code into subroutines (using the **SUB/END SUB** statements); like in QBASIC (which was released several years after True BASIC), subroutines can take parameters, contain variables strictly local in scope, and do not return values to the main program when they are called (using the **CALL** keyword). True recursion is thus possible in True BASIC. True BASIC is also similar to QBASIC with respect to functions (using the **DEF/END DEF** statements), which return values to the main program. The **MAT** statement reemerged to handle matrices, and commenting code (all comments begin with an exclamation point) was encouraged. Libraries of routines, using the **LIBRARY** statement, could be built and imported to expand True BASIC's flexibility, and graphics commands were powerful and intuitive. Encapsulation via "modules" permitted very large programs. And there was even mouse support.

Kemeny and Kurtz were especially concerned that True BASIC, which would be a direct descendent of Dartmouth BASIC built off of BASIC the Seventh, could compare favorably to Pascal, one of the most popular structured languages and the language that had displaced BASIC in the education milieu. To ensure a favorable comparison, True BASIC improved upon some Pascal constructs, such as automatically allocating memory with string variables and permitting early exits from loops. (Early exits from BASIC **FOR** loops didn't originate with True BASIC, but instead with North Star BASIC—which was designed for the 1977 8-bit S-100 bus North Star Horizon computer—courtesy of the **EXIT** statement. North Star BASIC had other notable differences with the standard Microsoft BASICs of the time, including unique ways of operating with strings and arrays as well as different names for **PEEK** and **POKE**.) Also, unlike Pascal's strongly-typed approach, in True BASIC variables didn't need to be declared and numerical types could be "mixed." But learning programming using True BASIC might lead to sloppy variable use later on, since there was no incentive to think ahead, spare memory, and carefully organize the specific variables needed for the tasks at hand. Plus, variable typing went back to the 1950s with FORTRAN; John Backus justified the practice this way: "…we felt that if code for type conversion were to be generated, the user should be aware of that, and the best way to [make him] aware was to ask him to specify them." Having variables suddenly pop up ad hoc in True BASIC code without prior declaration might lead to a milder form of spaghetti code.

True BASIC made its commercial debut in 1985 on the Commodore Amiga, PC (DOS), and Mac operating systems. The reviews were mixed. Like the QWERTY keyboard, whose reasons for sticking around were more historical than rational, adoption of True BASIC in place of a perhaps less logical or functional BASIC was slow to come. A 1985 article in *Byte* by Jerry Pournelle described the error messages and the editor as confusing. Little things, like the question mark (?) not functioning as a one-character substitute for **PRINT**, threw off the reviewer. (Also note that no version of Dartmouth BASIC permitted the colon to compress multiple statements into one line.) The barrier to True BASIC adoption was high; learning how to use the language required reading "*systematically* through the entirely terminally chatty [printed] manual. Don't skip." Yet paradoxically, in an interview in the book *Masterminds of Programming* (2009), Kurtz says that "[b]eginning programmers should not have to wade through manuals. Most manuals are far too wordy to retain the attention of new students."

The software's licensing agreement was also a target of criticism in the *Byte* piece: "The Addison-Wesley lawyers couldn't figure out whether they wanted to protect their product—product is a pretty apt name for the thing—by copyright law, contract law, or trade secret law: so they tried for all three," resulting in "schizophrenia." Even worse, Pournelle asks, "The real question is: Why do we need True BASIC at all?" After all, True BASIC doesn't *appear* to do anything that good old BASIC—i.e., Street BASIC—has always done. Of course, the reviewer didn't dig much beneath the surface, but the fact that he felt uncomfortable or unwilling to speaks volumes about the initial hurdles True BASIC faced. Why switch from (free) Microsoft BASIC or CBASIC, he asks, and make your life difficult for little apparent gain? Which gets to the heart of the issue. True BASIC was written with compliance to the ANSI standard, he notes, but "Why a standards institute would set standard so at variance with the versions of BASIC that microcomputer people really *use* is not known to me." Pournelle even obliquely accuses Kurtz and the BASIC standards committee, which Kurtz had a prominent role in, of collusion.

Other reviews, though, praised the product. "True BASIC is ideal for students and educators that use BASIC as a part of their various curriculum. It may even be suitable for scientists or engineers because of the rich set of math and graphics libraries," a reviewer in an early issue of *MacTech* noted about a later version of True BASIC. However, the one consistent knock on True BASIC was that it ran a bit slowly because "True BASIC isn't compiled to native processor code (so that it will run on True BASIC on multiple platforms), programs written in True BASIC are slower." True

BASIC, unlike the original Dartmouth BASIC, is built with a multi-pass compiler, and thus programs are not converted into machine code directly. The compiler itself was written in True BASIC.

A 1988 software review in *Info World* put it plainly: "True BASIC won't be easy to learn for an old BASIC hack because of its different implementation of many commands and statements. But the structured paradigm should be easy to adapt [to] if you've never programmed or if you have experience with another structured language, like Pascal." Especially difficult was converting older BASIC programs to True BASIC. "If the authors want to foster movement of the BASIC community toward the proposed standard, the PC BASIC conversion program should be bundled with the language."

Kemeny and Kurtz had arrived late to the party which they themselves had started, but which Microsoft and others had usurped. Plus, unlike Dartmouth BASIC, which Kemeny and Kurtz gave away for free in order to encourage its adoption, True BASIC had a price tag (it was Dartmouth students who convinced Kemeny and Kurtz to turn True BASIC into a saleable product; Kemeny and Kurtz started a company called True BASIC Inc. to get the ball rolling). True BASIC, therefore, wasn't quite "The Original BASIC," as its product catchphrase proclaimed. Plus, True BASIC wasn't loaded into any ROM—as the old ROM BASICs were—it was standalone software, so users weren't ever forced to directly interact with it. As operating systems evolved, versions of True BASIC had to keep up: "It has gotten more complicated with the advent of Windows systems," Kurtz admitted. "True BASIC on Windows is more complicated to use than True BASIC on DOS." But, Kurtz added in a different interview, True BASIC has endlessly expandable libraries and permits infinitely large programs, which Microsoft BASIC variants—including Visual Basic—do not. And Kurtz claims that True BASIC is as object-oriented as Visual Basic (which isn't entirely object-oriented).

Microsoft BASIC won the battle, maintaining its dominance in the face of worthy challengers like True BASIC, but it ultimately lost the war as Pascal came to be adopted as the structured language of choice in educational institutions and GUIs like Windows and Mac's OS displaced text-based operating systems like MS-DOS. Contemporary versions of True BASIC continue to be churned out, offering advanced features, bug fixes, and updated libraries for a variety of operating systems.

CHAPTER 16

∞

The Third Generation

As operating systems transitioned from command-line to graphical user interfaces (GUIs) and the programming paradigm shifted to object-oriented code, BASIC was ripe for reinvention one more time.

Steve Jobs' 1979 visit to the Xerox's Palo Alto Research Center (PARC), run by Bob Taylor and featuring innovations by the computer pioneer Alan Kay, has achieved the status of a modern-day myth; although Jobs didn't quite steal fire like Prometheus, he did lift the fundamentals for an ur-GUI: point-and-click (with a mouse, though Douglas Engelbart fashioned one back in the 1950s and demonstrated it and other peripherals during "The Mother of All Demos" a decade later) graphics, replete with icons and folders and a trash can. Jobs' highly refined sense of style and love of fonts—he developed much of his aesthetic sense in a calligraphy class at Reed College—allowed him to see the obvious that others failed to spot. "You're sitting on a goldmine!" he told them incredulously. "I can't believe Xerox is not taking advantage of this." (In fairness, though, Xerox also showed Jobs demos of Ethernet—networked Alto computers exchanging e-mails—and the object-oriented programming language Smalltalk, but he failed to be inspired by either new technology. Also, Xerox did try to capitalize on the GUI technology, releasing the Xerox Star workstation for "paperless office" businesses, but it had poor sales in part because of its hefty price tag.)

Jobs demanded that Apple's engineers reverse engineer Xerox's bitmapped GUI, building the Lisa (1983 release date) and the Macintosh (1984 release date) around them. "Good artists copy, great artists steal," as he famously justified his behavior, echoing Picasso. Since Microsoft had partnered with Apple on software projects such as Applesoft, Bill Gates had an early look at the GUI of the Lisa and the Mac, and he was suitably impressed. "The really unique thing we got into was when Steve Jobs came up and talked about what he was doing with the Macintosh," Gates recalled. "He solicited us to write a family of applications for that machine. And because of our background in looking at what Xerox had done with graphics interface, we were very excited about this design."

Apple's Andy Hertzfeld, however, suspected that Gates, far from being interesting in only writing applications for the computer, was gathering intel all in an effort to clone the Mac's bitmapped GUI and mouse layout. Of course, Hertzfeld was proven correct: only months before the Mac was set for launch, Microsoft held a press conference in Manhattan announcing the development of its own GUI, Windows, to be made available for the IBM PC and its clones. Jobs accused Gates, in person, of "ripping us off!" Gates' riposte, however, was more in line with the truth. "Well, Steve, I think there's more than one way of looking at it. I think it's more like we both had this rich neighbor named Xerox and I broke into his house to steal the TV set and found out that you had already stolen it."

Karl Marx once said that history repeats itself, first as tragedy, then as farce. Recall that Microsoft got its start by repackaging and revising another piece of software: Dartmouth BASIC. Then, Microsoft repackaged a clone of CP/M, calling it MS-DOS—a tragedy for Digital Research, from which it never truly recovered. Now, Microsoft rebranded the critical elements of the Mac's GUI as Windows—a farce that hurt Microsoft's reputation for years to come, even as it also took a significant bite out of Apple's sales. The first version of Windows was released in 1985. Although Windows underwent many growing pains, by the early 1990s came the much-improved Windows 3.0 and the software consequently became difficult to avoid.

Although QuickBASIC—and, by extension, QBASIC—had a menu-driven IDE, the language ran as an executable in DOS, not Windows. The story of how BASIC was first made available for Windows begins in San Francisco in 1952 with the birth of Alan Cooper. Cooper was rebellious as a youth, dropping out of high school; following a circuitous path, he nurtured an interest in software design and managed to snag an associate's degree and a job programming in COBOL.

Cooper soon, however, found himself restless, and decided to start a business software firm: Structured Systems Group (SSG). There, Cooper wrote, published, and distributed a number of commercial application programs. By the mid-1980s, Cooper had left SSG; he began developing more software, now with Microsoft Windows as the platform. He was especially taken with Windows' dynamic-link library (DLL) feature, which contained useful code that programs could call and share. Cooper was not impressed, however, with the Windows shell program, which interfaced between the operating system and the user. "Microsoft's original shell, called MSDOS.EXE, was extremely stupid, and it was one of the main stumbling blocks to the initial success of Windows," he said. So, Cooper set to work on a "shell construction set," a configurable shell design personalized for each user, called Tripod; he wrote the code in the C programming language. Tripod had forms, tools, and "gizmos" as well as a drag-and-drop interface with which to sandbox them.

In 1988, Cooper demonstrated Tripod to Bill Gates, and Gates was sold on the product. The Tripod name was changed to Ruby (no connection to the programming language), and Cooper assembled a small team of programmers to revamp and polish the software. By 1990, after a total rewrite, Ruby was ready. It came with a simple shell programming language; Cooper wanted it to be C-based, but Microsoft insisted that it be implemented with Quick-BASIC. Nevertheless, Ruby had a dynamic "gizmo" palette, a sophisticated front-end interface of tools and DLLs that eventually evolved into the custom control Visual Basic Extension (VBX) model.

Instead of integrating Ruby with Windows 3.0—giving it an improved shell—the GUI was shipped with a shell from another Microsoft software product. Cooper explains what happened next:

> The decision was made to delay shipping Ruby and to convert it from a shell construction set for all users of Windows, to a visual programming language for professional programmers by adding QuickBASIC. At first, I was very frustrated by Microsoft's decision, and argued against it. However, I was impressed by the power of the eventual product, and soon became an enthusiastic Visual Basic supporter.

In the first book ever published on Visual Basic, author Mitchell Waite calls Alan Cooper—who went on to win a prestigious Windows Pioneer award, one of only seven ever distributed—the "father of Visual Basic," a moniker Cooper has since embraced as his "one-line biography."

Visual Basic, which made GUI programming accessible to beginners, went through a number of iterations in the 1990s. The first version was released in 1991 for Windows (there was also a DOS release which was, in essence, a repackaged QuickBASIC compiler); in 1995, VB 4.0 allowed users to create both 16-bit and 32-bit applications, while VB 5.0, released in 1997, was only available for 32-bit versions of Windows, and permitted custom user controls. In 1998, the final VB was released: version 6.0, which allowed users to design applications for the then-burgeoning internet. All versions of VB had nonlinear event-driven programming—that is, some event (like a mouse click or keypress) triggered the software to execute some code associated with the event. Code could be tied to a variety of controls and components laid out on a form via the drag-and-drop interface; furthermore, attributes of the controls could be modified, both by the programmer during the design of the GUI and by the user, if permitted in the application, during runtime.

Putting aside code for manipulating the GUI, such as the `MsgBox` function (to relay messages on-screen; essentially, this is an equivalent to the **PRINT** statement) and changeable properties tied to objects, it's remarkable how similar VB code is to QBASIC code. Like QBASIC, there are Sub Procedures (i.e., subroutines), enclosed by the keywords `Sub` and `End Sub`; there are Functions, which return a value to the calling code; there are familiar keywords like `Dim`, which declare numeric and string variables (declarations are still optional) and arrays, as well as `If...Then` and `For...Next` and `While...End`, which all work exactly as expected. VB has no problem running recursive code (the QBASIC factorial function example relayed earlier will run nearly unchanged in VB), and it loosely conforms to the object-oriented paradigm of programming, where programs are built around objects. (Visual Basic .NET, the incompatible successor to Visual Basic 6.0 released in 2002, was strictly object-oriented in its approach.) Transport a late-1960s Dartmouth undergraduate familiar with BASIC to the year 1997, have him look at a side-by-side listing of VB code and Pascal code, and then ask him: Which one is BASIC? There can be no doubt as to his (correct) answer.

Visual Basic for Applications for Microsoft Office.

Visual Basic was also integrated into Microsoft Office in the guise of Visual Basic for Applications (VBA), which still serves as the macro programming language for the software suite. VBA is usually utilized to automate repetitive tasks in Word, Excel, or Outlook; it has become the means through which most people get exposed to Visual Basic code.

Although Microsoft products continue to be the most likely place to encounter BASIC (this is true stretching all the way back to the Altair), Microsoft Visual Basic was not the only object-oriented version of BASIC released. OpenOffice Basic, for instance, was a BASIC dialect that underpinned the OpenOffice (formerly StarOffice) suite, a software package positioned as a free alternative to Microsoft Office.

Blitz BASIC has its roots as a BASIC compiler for the Commodore Amiga line of personal computers, which were released in the mid-1980s. Like Integer BASIC, Blitz BASIC was designed with game programming in mind. Numerous iterations of the compiler followed, and as the software matured it become available for Windows, Mac, and Linux operating systems.

Other multi-platform, object-oriented BASICs include Chipmunk Basic, DarkBASIC, FreeBASIC, Gambas, GLBasic, Run BASIC (which is based on Liberty BASIC, a procedure-oriented form of the language), and Xojo. Needless to say, there are many options—perhaps too many.

CHAPTER 17

∞

Thinking Small

In a much-discussed 2006 essay published online in *Salon* magazine called "Why Johnny Can't Code" (the title is a play on Rudolf Flesch's classic book *Why Johnny Can't Read*), scientist and science fiction author David Brin lamented the loss of an easy-to-use, ready-at-a-moment's-notice BASIC.

Dismissing entry-level languages like Perl, Python, and even Visual Basic as inaccessible black boxes for a beginner—more specifically, for someone like his son, Ben, who was in the fifth grade—Brin longed for the days of a "software *lingua franca*," a common programming language, that effectively confronted users directly because the language was encoded in ROM—like BASIC was in the early days of personal computing. Back then, BASIC ruled the machine; there was simply no avoiding it. The weaknesses of that first generation of personal computer ROM BASIC implementations were in fact strengths in disguise. "[BASIC] was crude. It was dry. It was unsuitable for the world of the graphic user interface. BASIC had a lot of nasty habits." he admits. "But it liberated several million bright minds to poke [and peek] and explore and aspire as never before." Writing programs in BASIC allowed a user to trace the logic, the steps of execution, of an algorithm, to see that dots on-screen moved to tune "of math, and not magic."

The impetus for the essay was, in part, a recurring question of Ben's to his father: What was the purpose of those BASIC type-ins located at the end of sections of Ben's school's mathematics textbooks? BASIC, and students' access to it, had once been so universal that mathematics textbook authors took it for granted that teachers could, if they wished, assign type-ins as learning exercises; not only would type-ins enrich students' understanding of the mathematics, these students would also be exposed to a small dose of computer programming, too. But with no lingua franca, such BASIC exercises are all but extinct. (And with textbooks having a shelf life of perhaps ten to fifteen years, virtually no students are encountering old math textbook type-ins at this late date.)

What have we lost with the loss of BASIC? Quite a lot, Brin forcefully argues. Like the Greatest Generation who tinkered with automobiles prior to being shipped off to war and then knew their way around the vehicles they had to use in World War II, the latest generation of technical innovations were being brought to the public by programmers who had cut their teeth on BASIC. As an example, Brin quotes the tech artist Sheldon Brown, who, in an Electronics for the Arts class, worked with the Parallax BASIC Stamp, a microcontroller that has a BASIC interpreter called PBASIC stamped into ROM.

Another similar example of BASIC's early influence over a programmer, which goes unmentioned by Brin, is that of Linus Torvalds, best known for helping to create the Linux operating system. Torvalds' first exposure to BASIC came in the early 1980s as an eleven-year-old while programming on his grandfather's Commodore VIC-20. "My sister says that the first thing I showed her was the one that everybody starts with when you're doing BASIC: **10 PRINT**, and you print a string, then **20 GOTO 10**," Torvalds recalled. "And that's basically saying, print that string forever." Specifically, his sister Sara claims that this was Torvalds' first BASIC program:

```
10 PRINT "SARA IS THE BEST"
20 GOTO 10
```

But Torvalds disputes her claim—"because we weren't always necessarily the best of friends," he said.

David Brin ends his essay with a sensible plea: for someone to build a new, accessible BASIC. "It would be trivial for Microsoft to provide a version of BASIC that kids could use, whenever they wanted, to type in all those textbook examples," he writes. Something that wouldn't take up much memory, that would have built-in, easy-to-run tutorials, and that "maybe [would] even encourage many of them to move on up. To (for example) Visual Basic!"

Microsoft was listening—well, more specifically, then-Microsoft developer Vijaye Raji was listening. (He later left the company to join Facebook.) As a child, Raji was an avid BASIC programmer. He started on a library's Sinclair ZX Spectrum using Sinclair BASIC, and then transitioned to the more powerful Turbo BASIC. Those early childhood forays into BASIC left a mark: he decided to become a software engineer.

After reading David Brin's essay, Raji asked some of his colleagues at Microsoft: With what language did you start programming? He found that most said BASIC. Then he asked them: How will you, or do you, teaching programming to your children? There, the answers he received were mixed, ranging from high-level programming languages like Python and Ruby to event-driven programming like Alice and Scratch to sheer confusion; several employees even took a hard line against teaching BASIC, regardless of whether they had a better suggestion, underscoring an obvious point: not everyone shared in the nostalgia for unstructured BASIC. (By the way, Kemeny and Kurtz took issue with calling line-numbered BASIC "unstructured" since it was technically possible to give these programs a semblance of structure; perhaps, therefore, we should think of "unstructured" as a relative term, rather than an absolute one.) But Raji was nostalgic, saying that "we've lost the charm of [boot to] BASIC as we've gone on to higher, more sophisticated languages." Raji questioning his fellow employees "got me thinking as to why isn't there a 'Small' variant of BASIC that brings the simplicity of the original language to the modern day," he wrote. So, he did research on how young people learn programming today; what he discovered is that most students, when they arrive at college, get introduced to Java, an object-oriented language.

Raji decided to build a new BASIC in his spare time—he called it Small Basic—with the express purpose of keeping things simple and inviting for the beginner. There had to be a "very small set of concepts" with Small Basic; "it's imperative, it starts from the top and it goes to the bottom, and there are branching instructions that you can use to tell the program what to do. You don't have to worry about object-oriented programming, or hiding, encapsulating, or inheritance.... [things] not intended for the beginners and the kids," he explained in an interview. "[Small Basic] is intentionally limited." If these young users want more capabilities and fewer limitations, this will hopefully spur them on to investigate more powerful programming languages, and Small Basic will have served its purpose of sparking an early interest in coding.

In addition, Raji said, the ability to download pictures from social media and import simple libraries updates and freshens BASIC for today's young people, who have their hand in a constant barrage of online multimedia; it would be foolish to only offer them text-based programming.

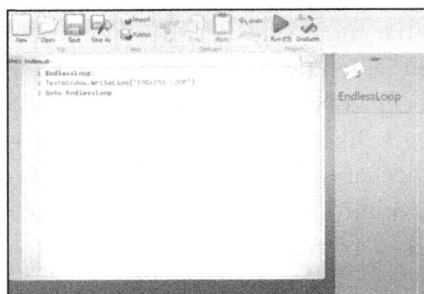

Small Basic for Windows.

The first version of Small Basic, a Microsoft .NET language, was released in 2008. Raji kept the language small: there are only fourteen keywords, the same number available in BASIC the First. But unlike BASIC the First, much of Small Basic conforms to an object-oriented paradigm, and Small Basic looks like a modern, GUI-intensive development environment (including a feature called "Intellisense," which dynamically presents properties and methods of objects). For example, the standard (built-in) library includes a Turtle graphics class, harking back to the LOGO programming language. For instance, the statements

```
Turtle.Move(50)
Turtle.TurnLeft()
```

moves the Turtle (the cursor) 50 pixels and then turns it 90 degrees to the left, the code itself looking like a modernist reinterpretation of an old concept. (LOGO is a product of the days before display monitors; in place of drawing on a screen, when the turtle was commanded to move using LOGO code, the computer signaled a robotic "turtle" to move on the floor in step with the commands.) There is also a Small Basic Math class with a number of methods including absolute value, square root, trigonometric functions, and pseudorandom number generation. Third-party libraries are also supported.

Small Basic allows for string, numeric, and Boolean (true or false) data types, although variables do not need to be declared. Arrays of multiple dimensions are also possible, and all arrays are zero-indexed (i.e., the first element is the zeroth index). Small Basic even includes an online publishing component; any program created in Small Basic can be uploaded online, at which point the user is given an ID number to access and run the code within an internet browser. In addition, Small Basic code can be transferred to Visual Basic.

And, in a decidedly old-school throwback, Kidware Software received permission to republish David Ahl's *BASIC Computer Games* (2010), updated with Small Basic versions of the original games. This time, however, the book is in an electronic format, with no typing of program lines necessary.

Small Basic isn't perfect. For instance, it is oftentimes cumbersome to complete the simplest of tasks. Whereas a first-generation BASIC statement to print out text might look like this:

```
PRINT "ALTAIR 8800"
```

Small Basic's looks like this:

```
TextWindow.WriteLine("ALTAIR 8800")
```

although, to be fair, the Small Basic code is of a piece with modern programming, which is the point: Small Basic should serve as a stepping stone to today's programming environments, not yesterday's, if it is truly to follow in the footsteps of past BASICs.

But Small Basic has other systemic issues. Unlike in QBASIC and Visual Basic, variables cannot technically be passed to subroutines because all variables are automatically global in scope. The positives of this approach are highlighted by Majed Marji and Ed Price, authors of *Learn to Program with Small Basic: An Introduction to*

Programming with Games, Art, Science, and Math (2016): "This feature is helpful because it lets you define variables just when you need them (instead of having to put all your variables at the top of your program)." Which doesn't make sense, since Small Basic makes use of predefined objects that have methods—and many of these methods have parameters. On the website I Programmer, author Mike James gets to the heart of this contradiction:

> For example, [the method to produce text output is:]
>
> ```
> TextWindow.WriteLine(MyString)
> ```
>
> so this makes it necessary to at least introduce parameters if only in a limited way. More importantly without the ability to pass parameters and obtain return values subroutines don't really have the power that is needed to convince the beginner that they are a really good idea. In short you better prepare a good answer to "why use a subroutine when all the variables are global."

Just as in unstructured versions of BASIC, such as GW-BASIC, subroutine labels in Small Basic serve as mere bookmarks to informal blocks of code, not functional subroutines. Thus, appearances can be deceiving: Small Basic might look like a modern language, but the resemblance is—rather surprisingly—only skin deep in many respects.

Furthermore, Small Basic didn't really solve the dilemma Brin presented in "Why Johnny Can't Code," because unlike ROM BASICs in their heyday, Small Basic isn't ubiquitous, requires multiple steps to download and install, and doesn't force you to ever use it. In fact, Brin believes many people missed the point of his essay; for some, his words only stoked the passions of the BASIC faithful—and the BASIC haters. "I have never received as much hate mail as I got for that article, not even for my infamous attacks on *Star Wars*," he later said.

> It was almost entirely from people who missed the point, with all the rage directed at Basic. Let me be clear that I am not defending Basic. It was a primitive line-coding program, but everyone had it. Textbooks had exercises written in Basic, and teachers could count on a large fraction of their students being able to perform those assignments.

But the BASIC of today has become optional, a niche product powered by the fumes of nostalgia; just as broadcasters can no longer count on audiences watching one of three networks (NBC, CBS, or ABC) due to the mass proliferation of cable channels and online media, mathematics textbook authors can no longer count on students having access to BASIC. (Although, it is perhaps puzzling that type-in programs in older textbooks weren't reformatted to work with TI-BASIC, the simple BASIC implementation available on the ubiquitous Texas Instruments graphing calculator series; although modern mathematics textbooks usually have sidebars describing how to use these graphing calculators, few textbooks contain program listings.)

Therefore, no matter how clever throwback implementations of BASIC are—and there are numerous brilliant ones online, in the form of downloadable and browser-based versions, some even inspired by Brin's essay (such as BASIC-256); in fact, there are more implementations of BASIC available today (including online emulators for many of the BASICs mentioned in this book) than ever before—unless we agree to again turn over control of our operating systems to a high-level programming language like BASIC, the days of there being a programming lingua franca are dead and will remain so.

END
∞

What killed BASIC? Though there might be some legitimate debate inquiring into if the language is really dead, there can be no doubt that the brass ring of programming-language dominance slipped away from BASIC long ago. True, the rise of BASIC coincided with the age of personal computing, with a BASIC interpreter loaded into most ROMs, and these early users had no choice: BASIC loomed large every time they flipped the ON switch of their machines. But this doesn't answer *why* BASIC simply disappeared overnight, so perhaps the question needs to be split into two: What killed Dartmouth BASIC? What killed Street BASIC?

The answer to the first question is easy: Street BASIC. The original vision of Kemeny and Kurtz was corrupted (if you are to believe them) by compromised BASIC implementations that proliferated outside of the confines of Dartmouth College; by the time Kemeny and Kurtz tried to right the ship, it was mostly too late—Dartmouth BASIC, and its direct descendent True BASIC, had become largely parochial and arguably inconsequential.

But the answer to the second question—What killed Street BASIC?—is complicated and multifarious. BASIC was intended to bring everyday general-purpose accessibility to machines that were otherwise mysterious black boxes. The language was purposely designed to keep users insulated from the operations of the hardware (notwithstanding the hardware-dependent features of some Street BASICs). Yet once an accessible language like BASIC caught on it empowered others to view BASIC not as an endpoint, but simply as a mile marker on the long road of progress. Why, they wondered, do we have to write a program *every single time* we wish to perform complex financial calculations or organize and summarize data? Can't there be a way to automate common tasks and thereby *further* insulate everyday users from the operations of the computer—to, in essence, fashion an even *higher*-level language?

The advent of the electronic spreadsheet (and to a lesser extent word processing and database applications) answered these questions with a resounding yes. When Dan Bricklin and Bob Frankston met at MIT in the early 1970s, both were working on the Multics operating system, a precursor to Unix. Bricklin, an undergraduate, had experience with APL (A Programming Language) while Frankston, a graduate student, had written a BASIC interpreter called MicroMind. Bricklin graduated from MIT, landed a job at DEC, and then left to work at a New Hampshire company called FasFax that produced electronic cash registers. Several years later, Bricklin attended Harvard Business School for his MBA, quickly finding himself drowning in a sea of numbers and calculations, and he started to dream about dynamically "'word processing' numbers so that [he] could recalculate them with a new assumption—say, 12 percent instead of 10 percent."

> My image was based on a calculator with a mouse and a heads-up display like a fighter plane so you could see the numbers. I realized you could do it with a video screen (projection TV) and a mouse—some kind of a personal computer device. There weren't many personal computers in those days, but I knew it could be done. I decided that when I got out of school, I'd develop this electronic blackboard for numbers and try to sell it.

Bricklin discussed his idea with Frankston, who was enthusiastic. Not everyone shared Frankston's enthusiasm, however; in particular, Bricklin's Harvard finance professor discouraged him from proceeding with the project. Nonetheless, Bricklin and Frankston rented a nearby basement office that had access to time-sharing. During the day, people in the office were developing the Ada programming language; but at night, Frankston coded, handing off the results to Bricklin after his classes finished the next afternoon. The setup quickly proving to be inconvenient, Bricklin and Frankston decided to obtain their own time-sharing system.

Although, as Frankston noted in an interview with *Byte* magazine, the spreadsheet concept wasn't anything new—"Companies used two to three rooms of blackboards or rolls of paper to do their production planning as rows and columns"—Bricklin's transference of that rows-and-columns concept to a dynamic visual display was a new idea. To see how their spreadsheet concept might work, Bricklin at first coded a prototype in BASIC on the Apple II. But it was too slow and a memory hog, so they rewrote the code in machine language. And the "visible calculator"—or VisiCalc—was born. Change a number in a cell and all the other cells' contents were automatically recalculated. As Thomas Kurtz remarked, "[A] lot of the stuff we based on BASIC at Dartmouth can now be handled by other applications such as spreadsheets. You can do quite complicated calculations with spreadsheets."

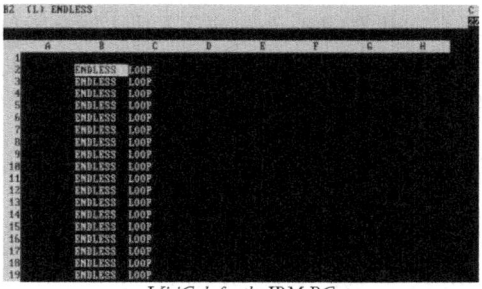

VisiCalc for the IBM PC.

The two MIT alum started a company called Software Arts, found a distributor, and polished their product, making sure to include comprehensive documentation. It was 1979. They placed an advertisement in *Byte* and hoped for the best. Once people, especially business people, understood the power of the product, orders started pouring in. People were purchasing the Apple II just to get ahold of the software; VisiCalc was the first killer app. The software was released for Atari, Commodore, Tandy, and IBM computers over the next several years. Over a million copies of VisiCalc were purchased. In 1981, Bricklin won the prestigious Grace Murray Hopper Award. But VisiCalc's dominance faded fast with the release of Lotus Development Corporation's Lotus 1-2-3, a slick take on the spreadsheet complete with graphs and other advanced features. Lotus Development purchased VisiCalc in 1985. The next decade saw the rise of Windows and Microsoft's full-on assault on the applications software business; Microsoft Excel slowly gained on and then surpassed Lotus 1-2-3 in sales, bleeding the life out of the product.

It wasn't just that BASIC was rendered mostly superfluous by spreadsheet software (although, rather ironically, BASIC is still used in Excel in the form of VBA—usually for writing advanced automation algorithms—and in other scripting languages as well). BASIC was also by and large ditched as the programming language of choice by the software industry—not only because of its unstructured ways (which were corrected regardless with products such as True BASIC), but because BASIC no longer conformed to the programming paradigm. Software programming evolved from the lone renegade to the corporate developmental team approach. Kurtz had never worked as part of a development team; likewise, BASIC was developed with solo use in mind.

And BASIC was also abandoned as the language of choice in education. At first, structured languages like Pascal took BASIC's place, with the College Board's Advanced Placement exam following suit. Then, languages like Scratch that abstract away the lines of code themselves began to supplant traditional computer languages. Scratch, developed in the early 2000s at MIT's Media Lab, is a visual programming language that is event-driven and freely downloadable. Programs are written not through the use of text but by dragging, dropping, and manipulating graphical elements. Scratch, though hardly the first such visual programming language (e.g., EuroPress Software's 1994 *Klik & Play*; the co-founder of EuroPress, François Lionet, had earlier programmed—what else?—BASIC interpreters: STOS BASIC for the Atari ST and AMOS BASIC for the Commodore Amiga), has become the most popular.

Spreadsheets and applications software further idiot-proofing computers, the language not conforming to the development-team paradigm, the College Board choosing a subset of Pascal as the AP Computer Science course's testable language, visual programming languages effectively idiot-proofing programming, and Kemeny and Kurtz publicly disowning the many dialects of BASIC along with computer scientists such as Edsger Dijkstra finding nothing to love about *any* BASIC—all these things conspired together in a perfect storm, killing off Street BASIC. Put simply, BASIC, whether of the

Dartmouth or the Street variety, whether unstructured or structured or visual or object-oriented, just isn't necessary—isn't *indispensable*—as it once was anymore. And that, quite simply, is what killed the language.

BASIC succeeded beyond Kemeny and Kurtz's wildest expectations, even if the language didn't always take forms of which they approved. On April 30, 2014, Dartmouth College threw BASIC a fiftieth-birthday party bash for the ages. The celebration was divided into three parts: "The Past," "The Present," and "The Future." Kicking off "The Past" was an official documentary, called *The Birth of BASIC*, that was screened for the attendees; afterward, a panel discussion in the Dartmouth Hood Museum of Art's Hood Auditorium commenced with Jennifer Kemeny (the daughter of John Kemeny and a Dartmouth alumna), Thomas Kurtz, and John McGeachie and a number of other then-undergraduates who had helped midwife BASIC. A distinguished chair professorship named for Thomas Kurtz was announced. For "The Present," the attendees flocked to the Hopkins Center for the Arts' Top of the Hop where they were treated to interactive computing demonstrations by Dartmouth undergrads. Finally, "The Future" moved attendees to Hopkins' Moore Theater for another panel discussion, this time with MIT's Daniela Rus, director of the Computer Science and Artificial Intelligence Laboratory, Google's Michael Jones, and Intel's Brian David Johnson, all of them repeatedly stressing how significant a role BASIC played in the history of computing.

If only for one more day, BASIC was again alive and well.

RESOURCES

∞

What follows is a list of the key resources that were used for researching and writing this book. For online materials, in addition to associated websites, the authors, dates, and source publications are provided (if available).

Books

Back to BASIC: The History, Corruption, and Future of the Language **(1985; Addison-Wesley—Reading, Pennsylvania) by John G. Kemeny and Thomas E. Kurtz.** An indispensable resource on the thinking of the co-creators of BASIC, this book documents the early history of the language but was written primarily as an advertisement for a then-new implementation of Dartmouth BASIC called True BASIC.

Bad Choices: How Algorithms Can Help You Think Smarter and Live Happier **(2017; Viking—New York) by Ali Almossawi.** A fascinating look at computer algorithms, illustrated with real-world examples.

BASIC Programming and Applications **(1976; Allyn and Bacon—Boston) by C. Joseph Sass and** ***BASIC: The Time-Sharing Language*** **(1975; Wm. C. Brown—Dubuque, Iowa) by Nesa L'Abbe Wu.** Two concise guides to using BASIC on time-sharing systems.

CoCo: The Colorful History of Tandy's Underdog Computer **(2014; CRC Press—Boca Raton, Florida) by Boisy G. Pitre and Bill Loguidice.** The definitive guide to the development of the TRS-80 Color Computer; the stories behind the 1977 Trinity (the Apple II, Commodore PET, and TRS-80) as well as the Tandy Corporation are covered in detail.

Code: The Hidden Language of Computer Hardware and Software **(2000; Microsoft Press—Redmond, Washington) by Charles Petzold.** A fascinating examination of the history behind computer hardware and software, from the earliest relay machines to modern programming languages and operating systems.

Computer Monsters **(1984; Scholastic—New York) by Stephen Manes and Paul Somerson.** A prototypical book of BASIC type-ins.

The Computer Storybooks of Stuart and Donna Paltrowitz **(mid-1980s; Tribeca Communications—New York).** A series of books requiring readers to type in BASIC programs to follow the narrative.

Gödel, Escher, Bach: An Eternal Golden Braid **(1979; Basic Books—New York) by Douglas Hofstadter.** A multidisciplinary introduction to mathematical proof and computer science.

The GW-BASIC Reference (1990; Osborne McGraw-Hill—New York) by Don Inman and Bob Albrecht. Easily the most thorough guide to GW-BASIC ever published.

History of Programming Languages (ACM Monograph Series) (1981; Academic Press—New York) edited by Richard L. Wexelblat. Original interviews relay the fascinating stories of the development of a number of computer languages, including BASIC and FORTRAN.

How Computer Programming Works (1994; Ziff-David Press—Emeryville, California) by Daniel Appleman with illustrations by Sarah Ishida. An extensively illustrated look at all aspects of programming.

The Idea Factory: Bell Labs and the Great Age of American Innovation (2012; Penguin—New York) by Jon Gertner. The indispensable institutional biography of Bell Telephone Laboratories.

The Innovators: How a Group of Hackers, Geniuses, and Geeks Created the Digital Revolution (2014; Simon & Schuster—New York) by Walter Isaacson. A beautifully written treatment of the history of computers, from Charles Babbage onward.

Learn to Program with Small Basic: An Introduction to Programming with Games, Art, Science, and Math (2016; No Starch Press—San Francisco) by Majed Marji and Ed Price. A prodigiously illustrated guide to programming in Small Basic that is especially informative for the beginner.

Masterminds of Programming: Conversations with the Creators of Major Programming Languages (2009; O'Reilly Media—Sebastopol, California) by Federico Biancuzzi. Contains an up-to-date interview with Thomas Kurtz.

Mindstorms: Children, Computers, and Powerful Ideas (1980; Basic Books—New York) by Seymour A. Papert. An argument for teaching computer literacy.

101 Games in BASIC (1973; Digital Equipment Corporation—Maynard, Massachusetts) by David Ahl. The original, and most popular, book of BASIC type-in programs, later republished as *BASIC Computer Games*.

PC Graphics: Charts, Graphs, Games and Art on the IBM PC (1983; John Wiley—New York) by Dick Conklin. A book that explains how to take IBM BASICA graphics to its absolute limits.

"Surely You're Joking, Mr. Feynman!": Adventures of a Curious Character (1985; W. W. Norton—New York) by Richard P. Feynman and Ralph Leighton. Nobel winner Richard Feynman's first memoir, a must-read for anyone interested in an intellectual life well-lived.

10 PRINT CHR$(205.5+RND(1)); : GOTO 10 (2012; MIT Press—Cambridge, Massachusetts) by Nick Montfort et al. Taking a single line of code from BASIC on the Commodore 64 as a point of departure, this collection of essays explores various approaches to creative computing.

TRS-80 Graphics for the Model I and the Model III (1982; Radio Shack—Fort Worth, Texas) by David A. Kater and Susan J. Thomas. A book that explains how to take TRS-80 Level II BASIC graphics to its absolute limits.

Videos

The Birth of BASIC (2014), the official full-length documentary from Dartmouth College released on the fiftieth anniversary of BASIC's creation

https://www.youtube.com/watch?v=WYPNjSoDrqw

BASIC at 50 (2014), a short-length documentary from Dartmouth College released on the fiftieth anniversary of BASIC's creation

https://www.youtube.com/watch?v=gxo9LVIgOiI

The Computer and the Campus: An Interview with John Kemeny (1991)

https://www.youtube.com/watch?v=HHi3VFOL-AI

An Introduction to Small Basic with Vijaye Raji (2008)

https://channel9.msdn.com/Shows/The+Knowledge+Chamber/Intro-to-Small-Basic-with-Vijaye-Raji

The Basics of BASIC, the Programming Language of the 1980s (2017)

https://www.youtube.com/watch?v=seM9SqTsRG4

BASIC Programming on Old Computers (2015)

https://www.youtube.com/watch?v=vmjJiH5bRQk

Triumph of the Nerds (1996), a documentary on the birth of the PC industry, based on the book *Accidental Empires: How the Boys of Silicon Valley Make Their Millions, Battle Foreign Competition, and Still Can't Get a Date* (1992) by Mark Stephens (writing as Robert X. Cringely)

https://www.youtube.com/watch?v=sX5g0kidk3Y
https://www.youtube.com/watch?v=EiffgiRAYUI
https://www.youtube.com/watch?v=ZFUsYXZSMqs

Bill Gates talks about Microsoft and the Altair 8800 (1994)

https://www.youtube.com/watch?v=pqAg0GJLPGk

My First Line of Code: Linus Torvalds (2015)

https://www.youtube.com/watch?v=S5S9LIT-hdc

Superman and the TRS-80 Computer Whiz Kids: Victory by Computer—Atop the Fourth Wall (2016)

https://www.youtube.com/watch?v=uag6HAsKiIw

Articles, Essays, and Historical Documents

"Fifty Years of BASIC, the Programming Language that Made Computers Personal" (2014) by Harry McCracken for *Time*

http://time.com/69316/basic/

Dartmouth Computer and Information Science Alumni Profiles of John Kemeny

http://cis-alumni.org/jkemeney.html

John Kemeny's Brochure for the Kiewit Computer Center (1966)

http://dtss.dartmouth.edu/brochure/

"Jurassic Hardware: Steven Spielberg's Father was a Computing Pioneer" (2016) by Tomas Kellner for *GE Reports*

http://www.ge.com/reports/jurassic-hardware-steven-spielbergs-father-was-a-computing-pioneer/

"How Steve Wozniak Wrote BASIC for the Original Apple From Scratch" (2014) by Steve Wozniak for *Gizmodo*

https://gizmodo.com/how-steve-wozniak-wrote-basic-for-the-original-apple-fr-1570573636

An e-mail posting by Greg Whitten, former Microsoft employee (2005)

https://web.archive.org/web/20090505111548/http://www.classiccmp.org/pipermail/cctech/2005-April/042999.html

"Tandy Radio Shack Enters the Magic World of Computers" (1984) by David Ahl for *Creative Computing*

http://www.atarimagazines.com/creative/v10n11/292_Tandy_Radio_Shack_enters_.php

"That Stupid Time Superman Shilled Computers for Radio Shack" (2011) by Cyriaque Lamar for *Gizmodo*

http://io9.gizmodo.com/5835188/that-stupid-time-superman-shilled-computers-for-radio-shack

"A Theoretical and Empirical Comparison of Mainframe, Microcomputer, and Pocket Calculator Pseudorandom Number Generators" (1993) by Patrick Onghena for *Behavior Research Methods, Instruments, & Computers*

https://link.springer.com/article/10.3758/BF03204529

"Microsoft's Odd Couple" (2011) by Paul Allen for *Vanity Fair*

http://www.vanityfair.com/news/2011/05/paul-allen-201105

"BUILD YOUR OWN BASIC" by Dennis Allison for the *People's Computer Company* (1975)

http://www.ittybittycomputers.com/IttyBitty/TinyBasic/DDJ1/BYOB.html

Dr. Dobb's Journal of Tiny BASIC Calisthenics & Orthodontia, Running Light Without Overbyte (vol. 1) (1976)

https://www.scribd.com/document/320834068/Dr-Dobbs-Journal-Vol-01
http://www.classiccmp.org/cini/pdf/DrDobbs/DrDobbs-1976-06-07-v1n6.pdf

"Dr. Wang's Palo Alto Tiny BASIC" (1976) by Roger Rauskolb for *Interface Age*

http://www.autometer.de/unix4fun/z80pack/ftp/altair/TinyBASIC-2.0.pdf

"A Tiny BASIC *Star Trek* Program that Will Have You Zapping Klingons Till Stardate 29.35" (1979) by Ian L. Powell for *Computing Today*

http://www.tenpencepiece.net/blog/wp-content/uploads/2015/01/Trek-BASIC-Instructions-and-Listing-CT-October-1979-.pdf

"The Return of Tiny Basic: An Examination of the Language that Started It All" (2006) by Tom Pittman for *Dr. Dobb's Journal*

http://collaboration.cmc.ec.gc.ca/science/rpn/biblio/ddj/Website/articles/DDJ/2006/0601/0601b/0601b.html

"HP 9845 BASIC" (2010) by Ansgar Kückes for *The HP 9845 Project*

http://www.hp9845.net/9845/home/about.html

"A Timely Look at Peek and Poke" (1991) by Tom Campbell for *Compute!*

http://www.atarimagazines.com/compute/issue128/82_A_timely_look_at_pok.php

"The Complete History of the IBM PC, Parts One and Two" (2017) by Jimmy Maher for *ARS TECHNICA*

https://arstechnica.com/gadgets/2017/06/ibm-pc-history-part-1/
https://arstechnica.com/gadgets/2017/07/ibm-pc-history-part-2/

"IBM's [Don] Estridge" (1983) by Lawrence J. Curran and Richard S. Shuford for *Byte*

https://archive.org/stream/byte-magazine-1983-11/1983_11_BYTE_08-11_Inside_the_IBM_PC#page/n89/mode/2up

"Donkey" by Andy Hertzfeld for *Folklore.org*

https://www.folklore.org/StoryView.py?project=Macintosh&story=Donkey.txt

"MacBasic" by Andy Hertzfeld for *Folklore.org*

https://www.folklore.org/StoryView.py?project=Macintosh&story=MacBasic.txt&sortOrder=Sort+by+Date&topic=Management

"Go To Statement Considered Harmful" (1968) by Edsger W. Dijkstra for the *ACM*

http://homepages.cwi.nl/~storm/teaching/reader/Dijkstra68.pdf

"How Do We Tell Truths that Might Hurt?" (1975) by Edsger W. Dijkstra

https://www.cs.virginia.edu/~evans/cs655/readings/ewd498.html

"Science Teaching and Computer Languages" (1971) by Alfred M. Bork for the National Science Foundation

http://files.eric.ed.gov/fulltext/ED060626.pdf

"Programming Language Choice: A Positive Albeit Ambiguous Case for BASIC Programming in Secondary Science Teaching" (1986) by William W. Cobern

http://files.eric.ed.gov/fulltext/ED280737.pdf

"When Children Learn Programming: Antecedents, Concepts and Outcomes" (1985) by Ben Shneiderman for *Computing Teacher*

https://eric.ed.gov/?id=EJ314171

"Atari BASIC: The Good, the Bad, and the Ugly"

https://web.archive.org/web/20070524044410/http://www3.sympatico.ca/maury/other_stuff/atari_basic.html

"Getting Down to BASICs" (1986) in *Compute!*

http://www.atarimagazines.com/compute/issue74/getting_down_to_basics.php

"PCs, Peripherals, Programs, and People" (1985) by Jerry Pournelle in *Byte*

https://archive.org/stream/byte-magazine-1985-09/1985_09_BYTE_10-09_Homebrewing#page/n329/mode/2up

"Potentially Powerful Language Comes Up Short" (1988) by Mike Todd for *Info World*

https://books.google.com/books?id=mDoEAAAAMBAJ&pg=PA78&lpg=PA78&dq=TRUE+BASIC+review&source=bl&ots=MD1b4YLEFZ&sig=0OZFABxAnJIFRlnpEQnvCrSegAM&hl=en&sa=X&ved=0ahUKEwjXoqLt8KbVVDdz4KHX3eAl84ChDoAQgqMAE#v=onepage&q=TRUE%20BASIC%20review&f=true

"The Return of True BASIC" (vol. 8, issue 3) by Dave Kelly for *MacTech*

http://www.mactech.com/articles/mactech/Vol.08/08.03/TrueBASICReturns/index.html

Profile of Alan Cooper by Hansen Hsu for the Computer History Museum (2017)

http://www.computerhistory.org/atchm/2017-chm-fellow-alan-cooper-father-of-visual-basic/

"Why I am Called 'The Father of Visual Basic'" (1996) by Alan Cooper

https://www.cooper.com/alan/father_of_vb.html

"Why Johnny Can't Code" (2006) by David Brin for *Salon*

http://www.salon.com/2006/09/14/basic_2/

"How are Students Learning Programming in a Post-Basic World?" (2011) by Lamont Wood for *Computerworld*

http://www.computerworld.com/article/2509286/app-development/how-are-students-learning-programming-in-a-post-basic-world-.html

"Small Basic—The Programmer's Guide" (2012) by Mike James for *I Programmer*

http://www.i-programmer.info/programming/other-languages/5196-small-basic-the-programmers-guide.html

"Microsoft® BASIC Version Information"

http://www.emsps.com/oldtools/msbasv.htm

In Memoriam of Robert S. Zale, the founder of PowerBASIC

https://www.powerbasic.com/founder.php

"BBC Basic: The People's Language" (2006) by Barry Collins for *Alphr*

http://www.alphr.com/features/91575/bbc-basic-the-peoples-language

"Sinclair's 1984 Big Shot at Business: The QL is 30 Years Old" (2014) by Tony Smith for *The Register*

https://www.theregister.co.uk/2014/01/12/archaeologic_sinclair_ql/

The History of Sinclair BASIC

http://faqwiki.zxnet.co.uk/wiki/Sinclair_BASIC_history

"You're NOT Fired: The Story of Amstrad's Amazing CPC 464" (2014) by Tony Smith for *The Register*

http://www.theregister.co.uk/2014/02/12/archaeologic_amstrad_cpc_464/

"Ten Years of Rows and Columns" (1989) by Tracy Robnett Licklideran for *Byte*

http://www.aresluna.org/attached/computerhistory/articles/spreadsheets/tenyearsofrowsandcolumns/birthingthevisiblecalculator

"On Computable Numbers, with an Application to the *Entscheidungsproblem*" (1937) by Alan Turing for *Proceedings of the London Mathematical Society*

http://www.turingarchive.org/browse.php/b/12

"FORTRAN: The Pioneering Programming Language"

http://www-03.ibm.com/ibm/history/ibm100/us/en/icons/fortran/

"What is the Oldest Reference to PEEK, POKE, and USR?" from Retrocomputing

https://retrocomputing.stackexchange.com/questions/15872/what-is-the-oldest-reference-to-peek-poke-and-usr

"In Search of the Slashed Letter 'O'" (2013) by David M. MacMillan and Rollande Krandall

https://www.circuitousroot.com/artifice/letters/characters/slashed-o/index.html#use-by-mathematicians

"A Brief, Incomplete, and Mostly Wrong History of Programming Languages" (2009) by James Iry

http://james-iry.blogspot.com/2009/05/brief-incomplete-and-mostly-wrong.html

Interviews

Dartmouth Oral History interview with Thomas Kurtz conducted by Daniel Daily (2002)

http://www.dartmouth.edu/~library/rauner/archives/oral_history/oh_interviews_pdf/Kurtz_Thomas.pdf?mswitch-redir=classic

National Public Radio interview with Thomas Kurtz conducted by Joe Palca (2014)

http://www.npr.org/2014/05/01/308569793/dartmouth-celebrates-50-years-of-basic-computer-language

A National Museum of American History interview with Bill Gates conducted by David Allison (1993)

http://americanhistory.si.edu/comphist/gates.htm

A Tech Ed interview with Bill Gates conducted by Ari Bixhorn (2001)

https://web.archive.org/web/20070704104845/http://www.microsoft.com/presspass/exec/billg/speeches/2001/06-19teched.aspx

A *ROM* magazine interview with Bill Wilkinson conducted by Peter Ellison (1984)

http://www.atarimagazines.com/rom/issue7/interview.php

An *Antic* interview with Kathleen O'Brian conducted by Randy Kindig (2015)

https://computingpioneers.com/index.php/Kathleen_O%27Brien

A History of Computing in Learning and Education interview with Bob Albrecht conducted by Jon Cappetta (2001)

http://hcle.wikispaces.com/Bob+Albrecht

Pcopy! interview with Galleon conducted by E. K. Virtanen (2008)

https://web.archive.org/web/20080821183950/http://www.basicprogramming.org/pcopy/issue70/#galleoninterview

Manuals

The Dartmouth BASIC Manual (1964)

https://www.cs.bris.ac.uk/~dave/basic.pdf

The MITS Altair BASIC Reference Manual (1975)

http://www.altair32.com/pdf/Altair_8800_BASIC_Reference_Manual_1975.PDF

Itty Bitty Computers TINY BASIC User Manual by Tom Pittman (1976)

http://users.telenet.be/kim1-6502/tinybasic/tbum.html

Digital Equipment Corporation DECsystem-10 Monitor Calls (First Printing, 1971)

http://bitsavers.informatik.uni-stuttgart.de/www.computer.museum.uq.edu.au/pdf/DEC-10-OMCMA-B-DN1%20DECsystem10%20Monitor%20Calls.pdf

Digital Equipment Corporation RSTS/E System Manager's Guide (1974)

http://www.bitsavers.org/pdf/dec/pdp11/rsts/V05/DEC-11-ORSMC-A-D_sMgr_Mar75.pdf

Microsoft BASIC-80 Reference Manual

http://www.classiccmp.org/cini/pdf/Microsoft/mbasic.pdf

Apple II (Integer) BASIC Programming Manual by Jef Raskin (1978)

http://www.classiccmp.org/cini/pdf/Apple/Apple%20II%20Basic%20Programming%20Manual.pdf

BASIC Programming Game Program Instructions manual (1979)

https://archive.org/stream/Basic_Programming_1979_Atari_US#page/n0/mode/2up

Commodore BASIC User's Reference Manual version 4.0 (1980)

http://www.commodore.ca/manuals/pdfs/Commodore_Basic_4_Users_Reference%20Manual.pdf

Atari BASIC Reference Manual (1980)

https://archive.org/details/atari-basic-reference-manual

Getting Started with Extended Color BASIC (1984)

http://www.colorcomputerarchive.com/coco/Documents/Manuals/Hardware/Getting%20Started%20With%20Extended%20Color%20Basic%20(Tandy).pdf

The True BASIC Bronze Edition Guide (2010)

https://www.truebasic.com/downloads/BronzeEditionv6Manual.pdf

Other Online Ephemera

The Dartmouth BASIC at 50 Official Website

http://www.dartmouth.edu/basicfifty/

The Disassembly of Altair BASIC

http://www.pagetable.com/?p=774
http://altairbasic.org/

***80-U.S. Journal*, a TRS-80-only publication**

http://www.trs-80.org/80-us-journal/

Ira Goldklang's TRS-80 Revived Site

http://www.trs-80.com/

David Ahl's "Simple Benchmark" program featured in *Creative Computing* (1983):

https://forum.powerbasic.com/forum/user-to-user-discussions/powerbasic-for-windows/5362-ahl-s-simple-benchmark

The Apple II History website, exhaustively chronicling the Apple II

https://apple2history.org/

The Blog of Vijaye Raji, the creator of Microsoft Small Basic

https://blogs.msdn.microsoft.com/smallbasic/2008/10/23/hello-world/

The BASIC program listing for *Dartmouth Championship Football*

https://math.dartmouth.edu/~doyle/docs/ftball/ftball.txt

The BASIC program listing for *Donkey*

http://drivey.com/DONKEYQB.BAS.html

The All BASIC forum and discussion boards

http://www.allbasic.info/forum/

ACKNOWLEDGMENTS
∞

Since receiving a Tandy Color Computer 2 as a gift for my fifth birthday and being subsequently confronted with the blinking cursor and **OK** prompt of a Microsoft BASIC interpreter, I've had a deep and abiding interest in the BASIC programming language—and, eventually, in programming in general, thanks in part to two computer programming teachers: Mr. Matt and Ms. Fricker, both of whom I had in elementary school.

Curious about the history of BASIC on the heels of writing two GW-BASIC books of type-ins, I procured all I could find—but was surprised that "all I could find" didn't include a book devoted solely to the story of BASIC. Sure, there was *Back to BASIC* by Kemeny and Kurtz, but (1) that book arrived in 1985 along with the public release of True BASIC, their software designed to take back the language from the unworthy hordes of Street BASICs; and (2) they mostly ignored the history and development of all BASICs save for Dartmouth's. Besides *Back to BASIC*, the best book treatment, by far, of the expansive sweep of BASIC's history resides in a single chapter of MIT Press's Commodore 64-centric *10 PRINT*, published in 2012. But BASIC's importance to the modern history of computing is too great to let its story be told in only one chapter—hence, the book you hold in your hands, which attempts to paint a fuller, more complete picture of this milestone language.

While ideally I would have preferred to have included a section on every implementation of BASIC ever written, tackling an expansive subject like BASIC demanded narrative choices in order to successfully pull together the many disparate strands of the story. Thus, the BASICs that ended up being covered in this book are the implementations I judged to be the most important to telling a cogent, nuanced, and comprehensive history of the language. I agonized over every implementation that didn't make the cut, but I wanted to make sure not to miss the forest for the trees. Whether my efforts have met with success, however, is for others to judge.

ABOUT THE AUTHOR

∞

Mark Jones Lorenzo, a teacher of mathematics and computer programming, is the author of two previous books about BASIC: *Ok* and *Not Ok*. He lives in Pennsylvania with his dogs.

Made in the USA
Middletown, DE
31 October 2020